Elizabeth

First published in the United Kingdom in 2017 by
Pavilion
43 Great Ormond Street
London
WC1N 3HZ

See page 157 for full Picture Credits

ISBN 978-1-91159-507-6

A CIP catalogue record for this book is available from the British Library.

10 9 8 7 6 5 4 3 2 1

Reproduction by Mission Productions, Hong Kong
Printed and bound by Toppan Leefung Printing Ltd, China

This book can be ordered direct from the publisher at
www.pavilionbooks.com

(Page 4) Princess Elizabeth photographed at Clarence House in 1951, in a dress by Norman Hartnell. US President Truman, that same year, described her as 'a fairy princess'.

Elizabeth

The Queen and the Crown

Sarah Gristwood

PAVILION

Contents

Prologue
Coronation: London
2 June 1953

(Clockwise from top) The Imperial State Crown is cut down to fit Elizabeth. The Anointing, the most sacred moment of the Coronation. Children in the East End of London prepare to celebrate.

It was, by any standard, a very big affair. Sixteen months of preparation, and Westminster Abbey turned into a building site as tier after tier of seats climbed almost to the roof. More than eight thousand guests, including the heads of state from seventy-three countries – so many, in fact, that the Royal Mews had to borrow extra carriages from Elstree Studios to transport them. More than two thousand journalists and five hundred photographers representing ninety-two nations; and so many soldiers, playing so complicated a part in the procession, that the ever-practical Elizabeth plotted out their positions using the young Prince Charles's toys.

At Edgington's flag factory in Sidcup, Kent, artists put the final touches to the cartouches to be used in the coronation of Elizabeth II on 2 June 1953.

Three million people lined streets decked with flowers from the Royal Greenhouses. Some twenty-seven million Britons watched the day's events on television, many of them on a set they had bought or hired for the purpose. But therein lies a tale, for if a monarch's coronation sets the tone for their reign, then there was debate about just what the tone of this event should be.

When Elizabeth's father, George VI, was crowned, just sixteen years before, the goal had been to present an image of tradition and stability. The Royal Family was desperate to put the abdication of George's brother Edward VIII, and his raffish image, behind them.

Now, the messages might be more mixed. Cautious voices in the royal establishment (the new Queen's mother among them) felt it important that nothing should change. But others – notably the Queen's husband, Prince Philip – understood that in the post-war world, the monarchy had to establish a different relationship with its nation. That the nation wanted to be part of this event . . . The modernizers' views had prevailed, which is why, as a cold grey day dawned on 2 June 1953, a 120-strong team from the BBC was setting up cameras in and around Westminster Abbey.

At the heart of the huge ceremony about to happen was one very small figure – the diminutive, twenty-seven-year-old new Queen. The Imperial State Crown had been cut down to fit her, and she had taken instruction from the Archbishop of Canterbury, Geoffrey Fisher, in the spiritual significance of the great ceremony she was about to perform.

The decades ahead would be marked by her religious faith, her strong sense of duty, and her anxiety to follow the rules laid down for her. But even this early in her reign, she was no cipher. It had been she who insisted Prince Philip should chair her Coronation Commission. Even this early, she had begun to understand that those rules would have to change when necessary.

Over the preceding weeks, she had been wearing the crown while sitting at her desk, to get used to its great weight. Prince Charles would recall her going in to say goodnight to him with it balanced on her head. She had practised her steps in the ballroom of Buckingham Palace with sheets tied to her shoulders, to simulate the coronation robes with their eighteen-foot train.

One of the first concerns in planning the coronation, after all, had been that of dressing the Queen. The sovereign required a whole series of ceremonial garments for the coronation – much the same as had been required since medieval times. She would arrive at Westminster Abbey in the crimson Robe of State (or Parliamentary Robe). For the most holy moment of the ceremony, the Anointing, she would be divested of this, and of all her jewels and other grand accoutrements, which would be replaced by a plain white linen shift over her dress. Then came a tunic of cloth of gold, with the Stole Royal and the Imperial Mantle – and finally, for the procession out of the Abbey, she would wear the purple Robe of State, or Coronation Robe.

Underneath all these ceremonial overgarments, however, Elizabeth would need her own Coronation Dress. For this she turned to designer Norman Hartnell, who was not only her mother's longtime favourite, but also the man who had designed her own wedding dress. He produced eight different designs and the Queen chose the last, the silver embroidery of which featured not only England's Tudor Rose but Scotland's thistle, Ireland's shamrock and the Welsh leek. (Hartnell begged in vain to be allowed to give Wales the prettier daffodil.) The Queen asked him also to add emblems of the Commonwealth nations, from Pakistan's wheat to Australia's wattle.

Hartnell also supplied the white linen shift, but the commission for the Robes of State went to Ede & Ravenscroft, whose records describe a Coronation Robe of 'best quality hand-made purple velvet', trimmed with Canadian ermine and lined with English silk satin. The gold embroidery took 3,500 hours and the Royal School of Needlework used a rota of embroideresses, working continuously so that 'never a seat goes cold'.

For the drive to Westminster Abbey, the Queen wore the Diamond Diadem made for the coronation of George IV – containing no fewer than 1,333 diamonds! – and the Coronation Necklace made for Queen Victoria in 1858. The necklace had subsequently been worn by three consort queens at their coronation – mother, grandmother and great-grandmother to Elizabeth II.

However, Elizabeth II was not a queen consort but a queen regnant – a queen who ruled in her own right. This was not the first time a queen regnant had been crowned in Westminster Abbey, but the process had not always gone smoothly.

When Mary Tudor was crowned in 1553, four hundred years earlier, the usual rituals had to be adapted for the first woman to sit on England's throne. She just touched the knightly spurs, instead of having them strapped to her heels, and as well as the king's sceptre she was given the queen consort's sceptre surmounted with the dove of peace.

When her Protestant sister, Elizabeth I, succeeded Mary, almost none of Mary's Catholic bishops was prepared to crown her. More than a century later, when Mary II

Norman Hartnell's design for the Coronation Dress featured emblems of all the realm of which Elizabeth would be Queen, from Scotland's thistle to England's rose.

was crowned with her husband, William, the Archbishop of Canterbury (who held by her supplanted father, James) likewise refused to perform the rite. Mary's sister Anne, who reigned after her, was so obese she had to be carried to her coronation in a litter.

Queen Victoria – England's fifth queen regnant – became the first to be succeeded by her own child. But her coronation had been something of a shambles, with neither queen nor clergy sure of the rite. The Coronation Ring had been made to fit the

The Coronation Glove presented to the Queen during the Investiture, made of white leather embroidered with gold thread, represents the gentleness with which a sovereign should exercise their power.

wrong finger and Victoria complained that it caused her considerable pain when the Archbishop of Canterbury tried to ram it home.

In 1953, by contrast, extensive rehearsals made sure that everything would go according to plan.

Elizabeth herself seemed calm that morning. One of her attendants said to her, 'You must be feeling nervous, Ma'am.' 'Of course I am,' the Queen replied, 'but I really do think Aureole will win.' Her horse Aureole was running in the Derby four days later, and the Queen's answer is usually taken as a sign of her almost inhuman detachment. But surely it more likely sprang from a refusal, at this of all moments, to share her deepest feelings with anybody. Because what lay ahead would be utterly fundamental to the Queen's sense of her destiny.

The coronation of a monarch requires six different ceremonial stages. The Recognition sees the Archbishop of Canterbury – for this is, after all, a religious ceremony – present the new sovereign to the congregation on all four sides of the Abbey in turn. 'Sirs, I here present unto you Queen Elizabeth, your undoubted Queen.' It was Elizabeth's own decision to answer their recognition with a half curtsy: the last time she would make that gesture to anybody.

She was seated in King Edward's Chair, used in every coronation since 1308 and containing the Scottish Stone of Scone, as the Archbishop of Canterbury asked if she would govern with law, justice and mercy, and defend the faith. She gave the Oath as she declared: 'I solemnly promise so to do.'

There followed the most sacred moment for the Queen – the one the television cameras were not allowed to witness: the Anointing. Divested of her symbols of status, in the simple white pleated shift, she was shielded by a canopy borne by four Garter Knights. The Archbishop anointed her on the hands, breast and head with holy oil, applied from the Coronation Spoon (the only part of the medieval coronation regalia to survive Oliver Cromwell's purge in the seventeenth century).

As the sovereign takes on his or her God-given mission, they become in a sense something more than mere mortal.

The four-year-old Prince Charles, safely seated between the Queen Mother and Princess Margaret, was allowed to watch part of the ceremony.

But those present noted how, without her rich robes and her jewels, Elizabeth's slim figure and rounded arms gave her a very human vulnerability.

Next came the Investiture, culminating in the actual crowning, when the Queen was presented with the symbols of sovereignty. She received the spurs and the jewelled Sword of Offering, while the armills, the gold bracelets representing sincerity and wisdom, were clasped on her wrists, and she was robed again in cloth of gold. She was handed the Orb, while the Sovereign's Ring was placed on the fourth finger of her right hand. She was presented with the Coronation Glove representing gentleness; with both the Sovereign's Sceptre – set with the great diamond Cullinan I, the Great Star of Africa – and the Sceptre with Dove.

Then, holding it aloft for a moment, the Archbishop placed St Edward's Crown firmly on her head. As the whole assembly shouted 'God Save the Queen' (signifying that she could now rule by the 'acclamation' of the people), in a deeply emotive and almost balletic moment, all the nation's peers and peeresses put their own coronets on their heads.

The new sovereign had still to take Communion, and to receive the Homage of all the lords temporal and spiritual in turn. The Duke of Edinburgh had suggested that the lords should be joined by a representative of the Common Man, but this proposal had been overruled. The Duke himself was the first of the temporal lords to swear allegiance. Prince Philip had ridden to the Abbey beside Elizabeth in the huge piece of gilded fantasy that is the Gold State Coach, but there could be no question of his processing with her through the Abbey. Now on his knee, his hands between hers, he swore fealty, touched the crown, and kissed his wife's left cheek. 'I, Philip, do become your liege man of life and limb, and of earthly worship; and faith and truth I will bear unto you, to live and die, against all manner of folks. So help me God.' He kept his word.

There had been real concern as to how the Queen and her attendants would stand up to the long hours of ceremony. She said they needn't worry about her. 'I'm strong as a horse.' But, just in case, the Archbishop had a flask of brandy under his cope. And members of the official party were given lunch – of Coronation Chicken, a dish invented for the day – before they left the Abbey.

St Edward's Crown is only ever used for the actual crowning of a new monarch. To leave the Abbey, the Queen instead donned the Imperial State Crown, set with the Cullinan II Diamond (the Second Star of Africa), the Black Prince's Ruby – actually spinel – which Henry V wore at the Battle of Agincourt, and the Stuart Sapphire. The Gold State Coach, in a procession nearly two miles long, took two hours to travel a circuitous four-and-a-half-mile route back to Buckingham Palace, all in the pouring rain. Though freezing, the Queen was elated as the ride ended. 'That was marvellous,' she declared. 'Nothing went wrong!'

The four-year-old Prince Charles, seated between the Queen Mother and Princess Margaret, had been in the Abbey to witness part of the coronation ceremony, though Princess Anne, not yet three, was considered too young. But in the excitement and

Three million people gathered in the streets of London to watch the Queen and Prince Philip drive to Westminster Abbey in the four-ton Gold State Coach.

relief of the return to the Palace, both children were seen gleefully playing with the Queen's train and indeed the crown. The official photographer, Cecil Beaton, captured some intimate family moments as the Queen Mother tried to calm them.

Before the first of the Royal Family's balcony appearances, Beaton took the portraits of the Queen herself that seem to capture the day. As a child, watching her father's coronation, the young Princess Elizabeth had written romantically of how a 'haze of wonder' seemed to hang over the arches of Westminster Abbey. Now the backdrop for Beaton's photographs suggested the same romantic haze of stonework, against which the young sovereign's face stood out in dramatic clarity.

The balcony appearances went on almost until midnight, the flypast followed by illuminations and fireworks, as again and again the crowd called for the royal couple. At 9 p.m. the Queen broke off to make a radio broadcast, relayed through loudspeakers to the drenched crowd in the Mall.

'I have in sincerity pledged myself to your service,' she said, 'as so many of you are pledged to mine. Throughout all my life and with all my heart I shall strive to be worthy of your trust.' It was the theme of the more famous speech Princess Elizabeth had made a few years earlier, on her twenty-first birthday. And it was a promise that – through good times and bad; through youth, maturity and old age – the Queen was determined to keep until her dying day.

Cecil Beaton's iconic image of the Queen in full Coronation regalia, uses the soaring arches of Westminster Abbey as a backdrop to suggest both the glamour and the solemnity of the day.

Part I
Apprenticeship
1926–1956

(Clockwise from top left) Princess Elizabeth with her sister
Margaret at the Coronation of their father George VI in 1937;
at her wedding to Lieutenant Philip Mountbatten in 1947;
and at the christening of Princess Anne in 1950, with the
Queen Mother, Prince Charles and Queen Mary.

'We Four'

Princess Elizabeth enjoyed a happy early childhood, surrounded by pets. Here she plays with her dogs at the window of *Y Bwthyn Bach*, The Little Cottage, a gift from the people of Wales.

Elizabeth (like Queen Victoria before her) was not born the daughter of a king, or even a Prince of Wales. It lent a fairy-tale quality to both their stories. Indeed, when on 21 April 1926, Elizabeth Alexandra Mary Windsor was born at 17 Bruton Street in London's Mayfair, the mere fact she could be born not in a palace, but in her mother's family home, showed how few ever dreamt this baby would one day be Queen.

Her father, 'Bertie', the shy and stammering Duke of York, was the second son of King George V, and the throne was naturally expected to pass not to him and his children, but to his elder brother, the charismatic Prince of Wales.

Perhaps a look at the recent history of the Royal Family might have given some hint at what lay ahead. George V had himself been merely the second son of Edward VII until the early death of his elder brother (the dissolute 'Prince Eddie') put him directly in line for the throne.

But at the time of Princess Elizabeth's birth, there was no reason to doubt that her uncle the Prince of Wales would shortly marry and have children. So although there was huge international interest in this new royal baby – although little Elizabeth would be taught to stand at the window in Bruton Street and wave across Green Park

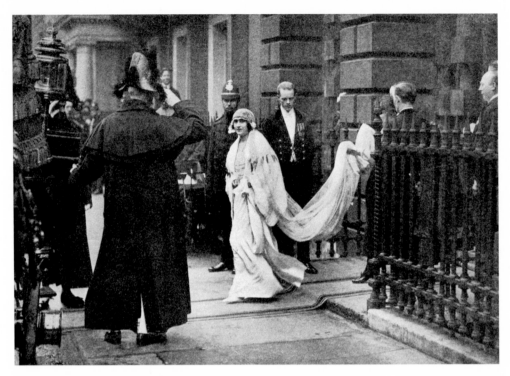

Lady Elizabeth Bowes-Lyon leaves her parent's house in Mayfair for her wedding to the Duke of York on 26 April 1923. Three years later Princess Elizabeth would be born in the same house – 17 Bruton Street.

to 'Grandpa England' in Buckingham Palace – the first decade of her life was one of comparative normality.

When her parents married in 1923, it had still been considered something of an oddity that any senior member of the Royal Family should be allowed to marry a commoner. But the First World War – which had seen the family change its name from Saxe-Coburg and Gotha to Windsor – had made the traditional marriage into the German Protestant principalities a less appealing prospect. And Bertie, like so many other young men, was besotted with the vivacious Lady Elizabeth Bowes-Lyon.

He had to propose three times before she accepted him. Nor were her parents, the Earl and Countess of Strathmore, enthusiastic – not being among those who, as Lady Strathmore put it, have to be fed royalty as sea lions are fed fish. They were themselves a family whose Scottish title went back to the fourteenth century and whose most famous seat was the immense Scottish castle of Glamis. (Indeed, by comparison the couple would find their first married home, the White Lodge in Richmond Park, distinctly poky.)

The wedding – celebrated in Westminster Abbey – was a huge and popular public spectacle. Bertie had been created Duke of York and the heartwarming style of the new Duchess was early displayed when – having lost a brother in the War – she began a fresh tradition for royal brides by placing her bouquet on the tomb of the Unknown Warrior. His mother-in-law said that the Duke was a man who would be made or marred by his wife, and the Duchess's influence would be an immensely positive one.

It was however three years before their first child was born, just weeks before the General Strike brought the country almost to a halt – a comparatively long interval by the standards of the day. After the birth, only the most discreet of announcements revealed that after medical consultation 'a certain line of treatment was successfully adopted' – code for the fact that Princess Elizabeth was born by caesarean section. In accordance with tradition the Home Secretary was waiting in the next room to verify the arrival of a new member of the Royal Family.

'I do hope that you & Papa are as delighted as we are to have a granddaughter, or would you sooner have another grandson?' Bertie wrote to his mother. Queen Mary declared that the baby was 'a little darling with a lovely complexion and pretty hair'. She was named Elizabeth for her mother. There was at the time no real thought of Queen Elizabeth I.

Nonetheless, press interest around the globe was such that the Australian papers dubbed her 'The World's Best-Known Baby'. (She would feature on the first of many *Time* covers at the age of three.) Even the fact that her mother and grandmothers had stitched her baby clothes was news.

But Elizabeth's immediate environs made for a secluded, ordered environment. Her nurse, Clara Knight – nicknamed 'Alah', a child's version of Clara – had been Elizabeth Bowes-Lyon's own nurse, and she stuck to the old traditions. Strict timetable, airings in the perambulator and an hour with her parents before bed. A Progress Book was kept, describing the baby's development – 'very healthy', 'vigorous', 'contented'. Adored by her grandparents, the nine-month-old Lilibet – as she became known after failing properly to pronounce her name – was left in

The Duke and Duchess of York pictured with baby Elizabeth after the christening ceremony. She quickly became, as one newspaper declared, 'the World's Best-Known Baby'.

Princess Elizabeth with her uncle the Prince of Wales, the future Edward VIII. He was a favourite of the young Elizabeth but his abdication would place great strain on her family.

their care when her parents set off on a six-month tour of Australia and New Zealand.

Winston Churchill, meeting Princess Elizabeth as a two-year-old, found already 'an air of authority and reflectiveness astonishing in an infant'. Others noted that she was unusually 'neat and methodical', as her governess put it – even getting out of bed in the night to make sure that her shoes were correctly arranged in pairs. That desire for order – that urge not to shake established patterns – would be both a blessing and a curse to her in later life.

What must surely have been useful was her early ability to separate one part of her life from another, to compartmentalize. She was early obsessed with horses. Her grandfather George V gave her a Shetland pony, Peggy, for her fourth birthday, and her stable of toy horses were each unsaddled and watered every night. But she also liked to play games where she was a horse in her own mind and, in that capacity, unable to answer any human query.

Soon after Elizabeth turned four her sister, Margaret Rose, was born. She had 'large blue eyes and a will of iron, which is all the equipment a lady needs!', her mother wrote in an interesting sidelight on how she saw her daughters' future roles.

Three had now become four – 'we four' or 'us four', as their father would always put it. The two sisters were even dressed the same; their father being anxious that Margaret should not suffer, as he had done, from feeling herself of secondary importance within the family. There may, even then, have been a sense that no more children were likely – the Yorks had not found procreation easy. But it didn't matter, since this was not supposed to be where the future of the monarchy lay. George V was only in his sixties, and his eldest son, the Prince of Wales, was hugely popular.

For the first years of their lives Elizabeth and Margaret were reared in not only an affectionate but also a cheerfully under-schooled atmosphere – educated to be wives, not world figures. They had, as Randolph Churchill said, no more education than was suitable for the rearing of 'nicely behaved young ladies'.

A new addition to the household was the nurserymaid, Margaret 'Bobo' MacDonald. The family now had the use of not only their London mansion (since destroyed) at 145 Piccadilly, but also Royal Lodge in Windsor Great Park. There, for for Princess Elizabeth's sixth birthday, was installed a thatched cottage built entirely in Welsh materials, described as a gift from the people of Wales and intended to showcase the skills of a nation whose people were suffering badly in the depression years. Y Bwthyn Bach, The Little Cottage, had a gas cooker, a fridge and every imaginable furnishing in miniature, right down to the packet of Epsom salts in the bathroom, and the princesses were encouraged themselves to keep it clean.

The rocking horse on which Princess Elizabeth and her sister were pictured riding in 1932, prefigured a lifelong passion for horses. Their mother had played on the same rocking horse as a child.

Elizabeth in particular also loved playing with the family pets. One photograph shows her holding a resigned-looking corgi like a baby in her arms. Her father bought his first Pembrokeshire corgi, Dookie, in 1933, and soon added another, Jane. There were also three yellow Labradors, a black Cocker Spaniel, a Golden Retriever and a Tibetan Lion Dog called Choo-Choo. The plethora of dogs, like the family's annual routine of summer at Balmoral and

Christmas at Sandringham, are among the many ways in which the adult Elizabeth would recreate the patterns of her youth – employing, even, some of the same people to educate her own children, like Madame Vacani, who taught the two princesses to dance.

When Elizabeth was six a governess – Marion Crawford, 'Crawfie' – was imported to take charge of the girls' education. She found, however, little interest in learning from the Duchess, who

Princess Elizabeth riding a tricycle shortly before her sixth birthday.

described herself cheerfully as 'uneducated on the whole', while the girls' royal father and grandfather were concerned only that they should learn 'to write a decent hand'.

What the girls' parents sought for them, Crawfie recalled, was 'a really happy childhood, with lots of pleasant memories, stored up against the days that might come out and, later, happy marriages'. The Duchess's view of childraising was in many ways an enlightened one. A note she wrote for her husband, in the event of her death, urged him 'not to ridicule your children or laugh at them . . . Remember how your father, by shouting at you, & making you feel uncomfortable, lost all your real affection.'

A possible downside was that at seven, Elizabeth had only a very modest hour-and-a-half of lessons a day. Nonetheless Crawfie – with the support of their grandmother, the well-educated Queen Mary – tried to inculcate an interest in current affairs, as well as some faint acquaintance with the world outside the palace. She taught the girls history, geography, grammar, literature and composition. She herself was no good at maths. Her work was made easier by Elizabeth's interest in reading . . . even if, inevitably, her favourite book was the autobiography of a horse, Black Beauty. The Archbishop of Canterbury, visiting George V on one occasion, was surprised

Princess Elizabeth and her younger sister were dressed alike at the insistence of their father, anxious Margaret should not feel inferior in any way.

to find the formidable King on his hands and knees, pretending to be a horse, while his granddaughter led him by the beard. When 'Grandpa England', as she called him, was ill, Elizabeth was brought to Bognor on the south coast to help him convalesce. But soon after George V's Silver Jubilee in 1935, it became clear that his health was failing fast. By 20 January 1936, the news bulletins told the nation that 'The King's life is moving peacefully towards its close.'

On hearing the news of George V's death his son and heir – the new king, Edward VIII, Elizabeth's favourite uncle – broke down in horror at the thought of taking up the mantle of kingship. He was deeply in love with Wallis Simpson, an American divorcee with a questionable reputation, already on her second husband. There had perhaps been insufficient concern in royal circles about the advent of Mrs Simpson. She was after all still married (and with perhaps another current lover to her name). She looked, in other words, like just another royal mistress – certainly not like a potential wife.

But when in the summer of 1936 the new King Edward took Mrs Simpson on a Baltic cruise, the world began to take notice. Mrs Simpson filed for divorce from her husband Ernest. In October an MI5 investigation revealed worrying connections with the Nazis. The British press were still maintaining a loyal silence on the subject of the King's affair, but the foreign press was full of the story. On 16 November, Edward summoned Prime Minister Stanley Baldwin and declared his intention of taking Mrs Simpson as his wife.

Through those weeks there was, wrote Crawfie, 'a shadow over the house' at 145 Piccadilly – albeit that the family's very typical reaction was to distract the girls with swimming lessons at the local Bath Club. Baldwin had told King Edward that the people would not accept Mrs Simpson as queen. The idea of a morganatic marriage was canvassed – a marriage by which Mrs Simpson would not become queen, nor would any children she bore inherit the crown. But everyone knew that if no solution could be found, the kingship would devolve on Edward's brother, Bertie.

The solemn portrait in the splendour of coronation robes reflects the change that had come to 'we four' as George VI called his little family.

In the first week of December the story broke in Britain, and the Cabinet rejected the idea of a morganatic marriage and on 10 December the King's irrevocable decision to abdicate was read to the House of Commons.

Interestingly, Baldwin's speech explicitly linked the ideal of monarchy – its role as the glue holding together the Empire – with its moral authority, and this perhaps was one of the lessons Princess Elizabeth would carry away from the event. Her uncle had chosen personal emotion over duty and the result was to place an intolerable burden upon her father, who wept when he learned he was now king. Said the Duchess of York – now Queen Elizabeth – 'I don't think we could have imagined a more incredible tragedy.'

On 11 December, the former King-Emperor, who would live the rest of his life as Duke of Windsor, addressed the nation via the BBC. On 12 December Bertie was proclaimed King George VI. That day the princesses hugged their father as he went off to meet the Privy Council. As he returned, they curtseyed to him.

'Does that mean you will have to be the next queen?' Princess Margaret asked her elder sister.
'Yes, some day,' Elizabeth replied.
'Poor you.'

Not many lives change at the age of ten, but Elizabeth's had changed forever.

In preparation for her father's coronation, Elizabeth's governess read her Queen Victoria's account of her own. She wrote her own account of the day as a schoolroom essay that is in the Royal Library today.

To Mummy and Papa
In Memory of Their Coronation
From Lilibet
By Herself

She had been woken at
5 a.m. by the band of the
Royal Marines playing in
the park and, too excited to
eat breakfast, rode with her
sister to Westminster Abbey
in a glass coach ('very jolty
but we soon got used to it').
She described their dresses:
'white silk with old cream
lace and little gold bows all
the way down the middle.
They had puffed sleeves
with one little bow in the
centre. Then there were the
robes of purple velvet with
gold on the edge.'

In the Abbey she stood
beside her grandmother in
the royal box, a dignified
little figure. The widow
of the last king would not
usually have attended the
coronation of the next, but
Queen Mary had expressed
a special wish to be at this

An intent Elizabeth listens to the music at a special
Coronation concert for London children, held at
Westminster Hall.

one. At the end, Lilibet wrote, 'the service got rather boring as it was all prayers.'
Sandwiches and lemonade before the long drive back, an appearance on the balcony
'where millions of people were waiting below'.

'I thought it all very, very wonderful, and I expect the Abbey did, too.'

War

Elizabeth was now heir to the throne – but, as a girl, she was 'Heir Presumptive', rather than 'Heir Apparent'. Any late-born brother would supersede her – and her mother was only thirty-six. (She would remain merely Heir Presumptive until the day of her accession, which is why she was never given the title of Princess of Wales.)

But even before the Abdication there had been – given her uncle's reluctance to marry suitably and breed – a discreet canvassing of the possibility of a Queen Elizabeth II. Indeed, her grandfather George V was reported as saying he hoped his scapegrace eldest son would never marry, so that nothing would keep Bertie and Lilibet from the throne.

The changes for 'we four' were instantly apparent. For a start, they had to move from their comfortably relaxed Piccadilly home into Buckingham Palace with its ninety offices, its fifty-odd grand bedrooms, its officers with archaic names like the Yeoman of the Silver Pantry.

'What, forever?' asked Lilibet, dismayed.

The girls would eventually find compensations, like the forty acres of gardens where they could row on the lake, and Princess Elizabeth found fun in walking in front of the sentry just to see him present arms. But whenever they went beyond the gates they had now to be accompanied by at least one detective and to refer to their parents always by their formal titles, as the King and Queen.

Their parents were much busier these days, and their father, at least, deeply perplexed. His family called his sudden rages his 'gnashes'. He saw himself as trying

George VI was determined that his heir should be equipped for the task that lay ahead of her. Princess Elizabeth looks over her father's shoulder as he studies state papers at Windsor Castle.

to steady 'this rocking throne', with always over his shoulder the ghost of his brother, the people's prince, the hero of the working classes. Perhaps Elizabeth would prove to have learned lessons from both her father and her uncle.

The question of a formal education for Elizabeth was now a more pressing one. George VI, he said in dismay, had never so much as seen a state paper before he became king. No one wanted his daughter to be similarly handicapped when her time came. From the age of thirteen, Elizabeth was sent to nearby Eton for twice-weekly lessons in constitutional history from the school's Vice-Provost, a noted authority, and thoroughly absorbed his teaching that the greatest strength of the British monarchy was its adaptability.

As her father settled into his role he would share his own experiences with her – a telling photograph from 1942 showed Elizabeth looking over her father's shoulder as he read from his red boxes of official documents. She had obviously accepted her destiny, telling the royal riding instructor that, 'had she not been who she was', she would have liked to be a lady living in the country, with lots of horses and dogs.

In some ways, however, Elizabeth was not given anything like the education of the queens regnant before her – certainly not the extraordinary Renaissance education bestowed on Elizabeth I. Crawfie remained the princesses' governess, hours of lessons were still lax, and the reports given out for the public concerned the cakes Lilibet was baking for children in hospital, rather than any intellectual attainments.

There was concern that she and her sister should not be too isolated, and so a special Girl Guides pack was set up in Buckingham Palace where she and the other patrol members – all relatives or the daughters of ranking courtiers – went trekking in the grounds and practised signalling in the long corridors.

But these and all other concerns were overshadowed by the international situation. Before the Abdication there had indeed been concern lest Edward VIII could be led into sympathy with the Nazi cause. (Recently discovered family film shows a child Elizabeth, with her mother and uncle, raising their right arms in joking imitation of a Nazi salute.) George VI had not been crowned a year when, in the spring of 1938, Adolf Hitler marched into Austria.

The Princesses (at Windsor for the duration of hostilities) joined the rest
of the nation in helping the war effort – knitting, and digging, for victory.

Soon Britain began preparing in case of war, erecting bomb shelters and digging
trenches. The princesses, like all children, had already been issued with gas masks
when, at the end of September, Prime Minister Neville Chamberlain returned from
meeting Hitler with the agreement he declared would ensure 'peace for our time'.
But the following March, Hitler's tanks rolled into Czechoslovakia.

As Germany continued to build up its armed forces, the Royal Family kept to
its usual pattern of a summer holiday in Scotland. As war was announced on
3 September 1939 and the King broadcast to the nation – as the Queen began training
with a pistol – their daughters were at Birkhall near Balmoral and it was decided
they should stay there, at least for the moment.

In fact, the first few months of 'phoney war' lulled everyone into a false sense of
security. While Princess Elizabeth conscientiously practised wearing her gas mask,

Sandringham Park was turned over to agricultural production during the war years. 'We four', as the King called them, inspect the ripening crops.

and studied *Jane's Fighting Ships* with her sister, nothing seemed to be happening. The girls came south to Sandringham for Christmas. In February they moved to their old Windsor home of Royal Lodge, described merely in official news as 'somewhere in the country'.

As food rationing was introduced, their father decreed that the girls' diet should follow the same rules as the rest of the nation, albeit that they had access to unrationed game and produce from the estate. They joined the local Girl Guide company – where fellow patrol members included a number of East End evacuees, who treated the princesses with less than the deference they were used to.

They were, however, powerful propaganda symbols for the nation at large. Much was made of the fact that they were remaining in Britain, rather than being sent abroad for safety – just as their parents were lauded for remaining in London even after Buckingham Palace was bombed while they were there. As the spring of 1940 wore on, and the 'phoney war' became a reality, the princesses were moved to Windsor Castle, where they would remain for the rest of the War. Windsor was, after all, a fortress – and there were plans for how to remove them to another, secret, location in case of invasion.

The castle had been stripped of its treasures (although, ironically, the Crown Jewels had been taken from the Tower of London and hidden in old newspaper in the underground vaults) and the girls, like everyone else, spent their evenings in blackout conditions and took their baths a mere three inches deep. They also slept in 'siren suits' in preparation for nights spent in an air raid shelter.

A welcome liveliness came in the shape of a company of Grenadier Guards sent for their protection. There were weekend visits from their parents – and, of course, the ever-present dogs and horses. But Britain was 'all in it together', and the princesses, too, dug for victory, and donated the miniature teapots and kettles from the Welsh cottage when the nation was asked to hand over its aluminium to make aeroplanes. A major part of their propaganda value was the idea that they were suffering like everybody else. As London was battered by the Blitz they feared for their parents, who were often driven back to Windsor at night. (Their uncle the Duke of Kent would be killed in a plane crash while in service with the RAF.)

On 13 October 1940, the voice of Princess Elizabeth was heard for the first time during the BBC's Children's Hour. 'Thousands of you in this country have had to leave your homes and be separated from your father and mother. My sister, Margaret Rose, and I feel so much for you, as we know from experience what it means to be away from those we love most of all.' The speech – written for the fourteen-year-old and carefully rehearsed – may sound a little stagy. 'My sister is by my side and we are both going to say goodnight to you. Come on, Margaret.' But the reception, on both sides of the Atlantic, was wildly enthusiastic.

Princess Elizabeth, with her sister by her side, makes her first radio broadcast.

The 1941 performance of *Cinderella* at Windsor soon turned into an annual fundraising event. The Princesses took starring parts, with Princess Elizabeth often cast as Principal Boy.

(Right) Elizabeth was only sixteen when, in 1942, she was made Honorary Colonel of the Grenadier Guards. A company of the guards were stationed at Windsor during the War.

It was not the only performance in which the princesses took part. The pantomimes they staged raised some £800 for the war effort. In 1942, as she turned sixteen, Princess Elizabeth was photographed signing on at the Labour Exchange as – under the national pressure to find workers – every girl was expected to do. Needless to say, no job in farm or factory was ever found for her – though in the same year she was invited to be Honorary Colonel of the Grenadier Guards.

As she turned eighteen, in April 1944, Princess Elizabeth was still in some ways treated as a child, and dressed identically to her younger sister. She was, however, given her own suite of rooms and a lady-in-waiting. She was now of an age where, if anything happened to her father, she would rule without a regent and, on his insistence, was made a Counsellor of State, able to deputize for him in case of his

THE TATLER
and BYSTANDER

LONDON
DECEMBER 30, 1942

Price:
One Shilling and Sixpence
Vol. CLXVI. No. 2166

Postage: Inland 2d. Canada & Newfoundland 1d. Foreign 1½d.

Cecil Beaton

H.R.H. Princess Elizabeth : Colonel of the Grenadiers

This year, on April 21st, Princess Elizabeth, the King's elder daughter, discharged her first public engagement by inspecting the Grenadier Guards in her capacity of Colonel of the regiment. The occasion was that of her sixteenth birthday, which also marked her entry into the official life of the nation. In this photograph she wears the brooch in the form of the regimental cipher, presented to her on behalf of the regiment, and the grenade badge of the Grenadiers in her hat. Shortly after her birthday Princess Elizabeth went to the local Labour Exchange to register for national service with others of her age group. Princess Elizabeth and her sister, Princess Margaret, last year presented *Cinderella*, the first Royal pantomime on record in this country, in aid of the Royal Household wool fund. A short time ago they gave another very successful performance, in *The Sleeping Beauty*, for the same charity, to an audience which included the King and Queen, villagers, and troops stationed in the neighbourhood

B

absence or incapacity. She gave her first speech in public when she launched her first ship.

Early in 1945 – declaring that 'I ought to do as other girls of my age do' – she persuaded her father to let her join the Auxiliary Territorial Service. No. 230873 Second Subaltern Elizabeth Alexandra

Early in 1945 the Princess also joined the ATS, the Auxiliary Territorial Service, learning how to drive and maintain army vehicles.

Prime Minister Winston Churchill joined the Royal Family on the balcony of
Buckingham Palace to celebrate victory in Europe on VE Day, 8 May 1945.

Mary Windsor learned to drive and maintain a car, take an engine apart and put it
together again. She recalled afterwards that she had never worked so hard in her life.

But she had been allowed to join the ATS only in the knowledge it would not be for
long. The War was drawing to a close. On 7 May the BBC was able to announce that
the following day would be Victory in Europe Day. The princesses celebrated VE Day
with their parents on the balcony of Buckingham Palace – and also with the huge
crowds below.

It was Margaret who begged that they might be allowed to go out into the ecstatic throng and, in the euphoria of the moment, their parents agreed. They were accompanied by a safe group of more than a dozen, including their governesses and a handful of Guards officers. Elizabeth, who was in her ATS uniform, pulled her cap down over her eyes in an attempt not to be recognized, but one of the Guards declared he could not be seen out with another officer improperly dressed . . .

Carried along by the laughing, crying, dancing crowd they went down Piccadilly, 'swept along' as she later said, 'by tides of happiness and relief'. They danced the Lambeth Walk and the Hokey-Cokey, sang 'Run Rabbit Run' as they linked arms in the street. They relished standing outside Buckingham Palace and yelling 'We want the King!' with the rest. They did the same the next day, and again three months later on VJ (Victory over Japan) Day.

The euphoria would not last. As the War ended, half the the British people expected a brave new world. The other half expected a return to the comfort they had enjoyed in the old pre-war world. Both groups were disappointed. Rationing was more stringent than ever. As even the King noted: 'Food, fuel and clothes are the main topics with us all.'

As the 1945 election swept Labour to power, and Churchill out of office, it was said that divisions between the different classes of society had never been more acute. But, ironically, the very discontent seemed to make the monarchy stronger – the one constant in a changing world; and an institution more closely identified with the people than with the aristocracy.

And for Elizabeth, nineteen as the War ended, this was a time of opportunity. A series of new adventures were about to begin.

Not the least telling change in her life is that she finally began choosing her own clothes, instead of simply accepting her mother's style. She was given a second lady-in-waiting, and also a male secretary and offices in Buckingham Palace and Windsor. She was opening buildings and awarding prizes, attending to her charities.

On Empire Day 1946, aged twenty, she broadcast an address to the youth of the dwindling Empire, poised on the edge of its transformation into the 'Commonwealth', which she compared to a free-growing and natural garden – 'what used to be known around the world as an "English Garden"'. The idea was to suggest a new freedom for the future – another year would see India's independence. But if the Empire had been built on conquest, a Commonwealth united for peace would remain a cause very close to Elizabeth's heart.

Princess Elizabeth was seen as the monarchy's, and the nation's, future, and interest focussed on one aspect of that future in particular – whom the nation's heiress would marry. 'That the Heiress to the Throne would remain unmarried was unthinkable,' noted Elizabeth's old governess, Crawfie (though the same had, of course, been said of Elizabeth I!).

She was by no means living in a nunnery. There were what a friend described as 'a whole battalion of lively young men' with whom she was happy to dance the night away. But it was a case of safety in numbers – she was allowed to go out in a group, never with one young man on his own. She now had her own car, with the numberplate HRH 1, but there was always a detective with her and a bodyguard close behind.

There was a small handful of aristocrats speculated as possible husbands for her – Charles Manners, the Duke of Rutland; Charles Fitzroy and Johnny Dalkeith, respectively sons of the Dukes of Grafton and of Buccleuch. But the same rules applied to them.

And, in any case, Princess Elizabeth's eyes were already turned in another direction.

Love and Marriage

It was in childhood, at various family occasions, that Princess Elizabeth had first encountered her distant cousin Prince Philip of Greece and Denmark. He, like she, was a great-great-grandchild of Queen Victoria. But Philip's dramatic and difficult family history was in stark contrast to the cosy domesticity of 'we four'.

Philip was the impoverished offspring of a discredited monarchy. His Danish grandfather had been chosen by the Greeks as their king at the age of seventeen, but was assassinated fifty years later. His uncle King Constantine had been deposed, and his father, Prince Andrew, exiled along with most of the family. Philip had been born, on 10 June 1921, on a kitchen table in a villa on Corfu, during his Uncle Constantine's brief return to power, but in 1922 Constantine had been forced to abdicate, and public hostility was such that Prince Andrew's family had to be evacuated from Corfu aboard a British warship, with the baby Philip carried in a cot made from a fruit crate.

His parents' marriage did not survive the strain of exile. Initially settling in Paris, Philip's father moved to Monte Carlo, while his mother was placed in a mental institution, suffering from what the conventions of the day described as a nervous breakdown, though more recent diagnoses suggest schizophrenia.

Philip was sent to school in England and raised there in the care of his mother's Mountbatten (or, as they had been in Germany, Battenberg) family. Under the aegis of his uncle Lord Louis Mountbatten, he prepared to enter the Royal Navy. And when in 1939, the thirteen-year-old Princess Elizabeth accompanied her parents to the Royal Naval College at Dartmouth, where Philip was a cadet, the eighteen-year-old helped to entertain the royal party.

The two exchanged letters from then on – and from that moment the idea of a match appears to have been in currency. In 1941 the diarist Chips Channon had heard gossip that Philip 'is to be our Prince Consort', and that that was why he was serving in the British Navy.

Curiously, Queen Victoria's husband, Prince Albert, had also been the candidate of a favourite uncle; in his case, Victoria's Uncle Leopold. Victoria's, like Elizabeth's, was to be a love match in which love nonetheless came by order, a personal choice made from a very limited gene pool. But in both cases there were concerns.

The question of consort to a queen regnant had always been a vexed one – the vexations that kept the first Queen Elizabeth a Virgin Queen. If Elizabeth I had married one of her own nobles there would have been the danger of faction; if she married a foreign prince, her country risked being subordinated to the interests of his. In either case, the popular assumption was that he would take over control not only of her, but of her realm.

Four centuries on the risks were smaller, in that Elizabeth II would not exercise the same powers as her predecessor. But in the 1940s (as in the 1840s, when concerns were raised over Albert's Germanic foreignness) the fears expressed in the sixteenth century had not entirely gone away.

Nonetheless, Philip was invited to spend Christmas 1943 with the Royal Family at Windsor, where he watched a zestful seventeen-year-old Elizabeth sing and dance through the annual family pantomime, after which the young people rolled back the carpets, turned on the gramophone, and danced till 1 a.m. It may – suggested Crawfie – have been then that her real interest in Philip began.

Philip in his twenties was as able (if abrasive) as he was attractive. He had an impressive war record, seeing active service and being mentioned in dispatches, and seemed set for a high-flying naval career. Elizabeth was obviously fascinated by a young man her cousin Margaret Rhodes described as looking like 'a Viking god'. And Philip – even at this surprisingly early point – told his naval commander that he might marry the future queen. It was, as he described it, the notion of his 'Uncle Dickie', Lord Mountbatten, who was fostering the idea every step of the way.

However, Philip was not part of the English aristocratic club, whose members were far from convinced of his suitability. Courtiers called him 'Phil the Greek'; some complained he was 'no gentleman', and claimed to see in him 'a Teutonic strain'. All four of his sisters had married Germans, several of whom had been active in the Nazi cause. And he was moreover like 'a dog without a basket', arriving for weekend visits to the British Royal Family in a third-class train compartment, without spare clothes, and writing 'of no fixed abode' when it came to signing his name in visitors' books.

None of which, to the Princess Elizabeth, mattered a jot. By the time Philip was invited to Balmoral in the summer of 1946, it was clear Elizabeth was in love. When she was a bridesmaid, and he an usher, at the wedding of Lord Mountbatten's daughter Patricia to Lord Brabourne, the looks they exchanged told the world what those closest to them already knew.

The Palace, that autumn, was forced to issue a denial of press stories that the couple were engaged and it was true – officially. In fact, some time that summer Elizabeth accepted Philip's proposal, though the King's consent had still to be obtained. George VI had doubts about Philip – about the young man's raffish reputation and rough edges, as well as about the over-active role the ambitious Mountbatten seemed to be playing in the affair.

Mountbatten had for several years been attempting to arrange Philip's naturalization as a British subject. That winter, he made sure that it went ahead. In the interests of becoming a less controversial consort for Britain's heiress, Philip would renounce his name, royal rank, his nationality, and in the end also his Greek Orthodox faith.

Still, however, there was no announcement. Indeed, the couple took care to be seen about together rather less. The Princess continued to dine and dance with a series of Guardsmen. Her parents asked her to wait until after her twenty-first birthday – and took her away on a long South African tour.

There was of course a political purpose behind the trip. Though for some years an independent nation, South Africa still acknowledged George VI as king. The British Government hoped the Royal Family's visit would strengthen Prime Minister Jan Smuts, and the English-speaking population of South Africa, against the Afrikaner National Party, which was pressing for greater racial segregation. Already, the royal party was distressed often to find black and white South Africans waving flags from opposite sides of the street.

But the trip was also in some sense a holiday, at least for the two princesses, who were filmed on the outward journey playing deck games with the ship's officers, with obvious delight. Because of the War, they had never been abroad and were thrilled by the vast open spaces, the animals, the Victoria Falls, the five thousand Zulu warriors who turned out to greet them – and, recalled Princess Margaret, the 'amazing opulence and a great deal to eat'. They had left Britain in the grip of a terrible winter and Princess Elizabeth, characteristically, wrote to her grandmother Queen Mary that she felt 'guilty we had got away to the sun while everyone else was freezing'.

Princess Elizabeth looked relaxed and happy playing deck games with the officers of HMS *Vanguard* on the voyage to South Africa in 1947.

The schedule of the royal tour was however gruelling – thirty-five nights aboard the specially fitted White Train. The King and Queen certainly found it exhausting but Elizabeth, noted the King's private secretary Alan 'Tommy' Lascelles, displayed 'not a great sense of humour, but a healthy sense of fun'. Fun and duty: Elizabeth, wrote Lascelles approvingly to his wife, had formed the habit of prodding her mother with the point of her umbrella when she showed signs of running behind schedule. Though both princesses must have found parts of the tour very dull, he wrote, they had both been 'as good as gold':

'From the inside, the most satisfactory feature of the whole business is the remarkable development of P'cess [sic] E. She has all P'cess Marg's solid and endearing qualities plus a perfectly natural power of enjoying herself. For a child of her years, she has got an astonishing solicitude for other people's comfort; such unselfishness is not a normal characteristic of that family.'

It was in South Africa, three days before the end of the visit, that Princess Elizabeth turned twenty-one. The South African authorities were never going to miss the chance for a public celebration, and she spent the previous day reviewing everything from cadet battalions to women's corps and civil defence workers, and taking the salute at a great march past.

Of course, the day was also marked by the live broadcast she made from Cape Town, and by a speech that has gone down in history. 'There is a motto, which has been borne by many of my ancestors – a noble motto, "I serve." . . .

'I declare before you all that my whole life, whether it be long or short, shall be devoted to your service and the service of our great imperial family to which we all belong. I shall not have the strength to carry out this resolution alone unless you join in it with me, as I now invite you to do. I know that your support will be unfailingly given. God help me to make good my vow and God bless all of you who are willing to share in it.'

Perhaps it is ironic that a speech written for her, and polished by Lascelles, should become in effect Elizabeth's personal credo. But it is one she was able to deliver with all conviction. It was an affirmation of the emerging ideal of the Commonwealth of Nations, and of the monarchy, the sovereign, as the glue that would cement disparate nations into a harmonious whole.

Elizabeth's youthful voice – high, rather cool – described also how Britain had in the past saved herself by her exertions 'and would save Europe by her example'. It was a reinforcement of that idea – set up under Victoria, reinforced under George and Mary – of the moral weight not only of the country but of the monarchy which represented it. In the years ahead this idea would prove to be something of a poisoned chalice . . . but for the immediate future, Elizabeth's thoughts were fixed on the journey home. She had, of course, been in touch with Philip throughout the trip.

Princess Elizabeth celebrated her 21st birthday while in South Africa, and marked the occasion with a famous radio broadcast. 'I declare' – she told the peoples of Britain's 'great imperial family' – 'that my whole life, whether it be long or short, shall be devoted to your service . . .'

On 10 July 1947, the announcement was posted from Buckingham Palace that 'with the greatest pleasure' King and Queen announced the betrothal of their dearly beloved daughter to 'Lieutenant Philip Mountbatten, RN'. To this the king 'has gladly given his consent'.

In fact George VI was still far from glad to let go of his daughter, while behind the scenes Philip and his future mother-in-law, representing very different ideas about the best path for a modern monarchy, would often clash in the decades ahead. But the wedding was set for 20 November, some four months away.

It was only since the end of the First World War that, after centuries of small private ceremonies, the Royal Family had begun to hold their weddings in public, as celebrations not only they but their people could enjoy. Since the wedding of Princess Elizabeth's parents, back in 1923, newspaper readers around the world had learned to relish every detail of a royal bride's dress, and huge crowds gathered to watch her arrival at Westminster Abbey.

In 1947, so soon after the Second World War, and with rationing growing ever more stringent, there were in fact qualms about whether a large public ceremony was really appropriate, or whether this wedding should again be held quietly, at Windsor. Some Members of Parliament did complain about the cost. But the majority opinion proved to be that of Winston Churchill, who declared it would be 'a flash of colour on the hard road we have to travel' – and it was clear the public felt the same way. The great Victorian Walter Bagehot wrote that a royal marriage was 'the brilliant edition of a universal fact', and so it seemed to an enthralled audience that stretched far beyond the UK.

When the wedding presents were put on display at St James's Palace, they included not only a sapphire and diamond set from the King, and a dinner service from President and Madame Chiang Kai-shek, but a rabbit tea cosy made by one Nurse Kirkpatrick. (The crowds who flocked to St James's presumably didn't see the Siamese kitten from two other district nurses in Wiltshire . . . any more than they saw the Aga Khan's thoroughbred filly, or the hunting lodge from the people of Kenya.)

A portrait to celebrate the engagement of Princess Elizabeth and Lieutenant Philip Mountbatten, announced on 10 July 1947.

Many girls around the country sent nylon stockings – a generous gift, since they were a rationed item – and these took their place alongside the five hundred cases of tinned pineapple sent by the Government of Queensland, and the rhododendrons from the Rothschilds' garden. A lady in Brooklyn sent a turkey 'because they have nothing to eat in England', and Mahatma Gandhi sent a tray cloth spun on his own spinning wheel – though old Queen Mary took it for one of his famous loincloths, and exclaimed at the indelicacy.

The wedding dress came from designer Norman Hartnell, and was presented as a triumph of British industry. The newspapers queried even the nationality of the worms who were producing the silk, wanting to check that they had not come from Italy or Japan, which had so recently been enemy territories. (Feeling still ran so high that Prince Philip's three surviving sisters, because of their German husbands, were not invited to the wedding ceremony.)

Hartnell's inspiration came from the Renaissance paintings of Sandro Botticelli, and the embroidery of blooms, picked out in crystal and some ten thousand pearls, represented the promise of rebirth and growth after the long winter of war. Press speculation about the dress became so hysterical Hartnell's manager had to sleep in the workroom, for fear of spies, and the Palace had to issue a statement that it was Princess Elizabeth's own wish to keep the dress a secret until her wedding day.

At the dance in Buckingham Palace two nights before the wedding, King George led a conga of royal relations through the State Apartments. The bridegroom's stag night, attended by his fellow naval officers, took place at the Dorchester Hotel. The King had arranged that Philip should be created a Royal Highness '& that the titles of his peerage will be: Baron Greenwich, Earl of Merioneth & Duke of Edinburgh . . . It is a great deal to give a man all at once, but I know Philip understands his new responsibilities on his marriage to Lilibet.'

The wedding day, 20 November, dawned cold and wet, but the crowds in the street were swelling until they stood fifty thick. Princess Elizabeth was peering at them out of Buckingham Palace windows, telling Crawfie that she had to keep pinching herself to believe this was really happening. Prince Philip ordered tea and coffee to be taken to the photographers waiting outside his windows at Kensington Palace.

There were some last-minute mishaps. No one could find the bride's bouquet – of white orchids, with a sprig of myrtle from the bush at Osborne House planted in Queen Victoria's day – and it was suddenly discovered that the double strand of pearls Elizabeth had planned to wear, a gift from her parents, was still at St James's Palace with the rest of the presents, on public display.

The bouquet was traced to a cool room, where it had been placed to keep fresh, and the Princess's private secretary leapt into a hastily commandeered car to retrieve the necklace in the nick of time. The bride and her father drove to Westminster Abbey in the Irish State Coach, escorted by the Household Cavalry. It was the first time their full ceremonial uniform and plumed helmets had been seen since the War.

Despite the splendour, the Archbishop of York, officiating alongside the Archbishop of Canterbury, said that this wedding in Westminster Abbey was 'in all essentials exactly the same as it would have been for any cottager who might be married this afternoon in some small country church'.

The wedding breakfast was an 'austerity' event for a mere 150 guests, with the main course a casserole of unrationed partridges. Each place at table carried a small bunch of white heather from Balmoral. King George VI in his speech said: 'Our daughter is marrying the man she loves.' Prince Philip, newly

Elizabeth and Philip beaming as they returned from their wedding in Westminster Abbey on 20 November 1947.

naturalized as a British subject, said that he was proud. 'Proud of my country and my wife.' Princess Elizabeth said that: 'I ask nothing more than that Philip and I shall be as happy as my father and mother have been, and Queen Mary and King George before them.'

The couple set off to spend the first days of their honeymoon at Broadlands, Lord Mountbatten's Hampshire home, driving to Waterloo in an open landau. They were accompanied by Susan, the Princess's favourite corgi, hidden (along with a handful of hot water bottles) under the rug which shielded them from the winter weather. Accompanied by Bobo MacDonald and by the Princess's personal footman, at Broadlands they found themselves attended also by a

London police constables guard the wedding cake. Because food rationing was still in force, the cakes were made from ingredients that were sent to the Princess from overseas.

number of unwelcome spectators, both press and public, who even climbed up on ladders to try to snatch a glimpse of the lovers. It must have been a relief when, for the second part of the honeymoon, they moved on to the Scottish fastness of Birkhall.

From Broadlands, Princess Elizabeth wrote to her mother of how hugely she had enjoyed the day. (Philip, she added, was 'an angel'.) In newspaper columns around the world, writer after writer described this as a fairy story. But, more importantly, it would prove also to be the start of the Royal Family's most enduring love story.

When Cecil Beaton photographed Princess Elizabeth in 1945, the lush romanticism of the image belies the fact she was wearing a pre-war Hartnell dress of her mother's – even royalty was not exempt from the clothes rationing of the War!

The King wrote later to his daughter that he had been proud and thrilled as he led her down the long aisle of the Abbey, but that when he gave her hand to the Archbishop, 'I felt I had lost something very precious.' He added, 'You were so calm and composed during the Service & said your words with such conviction, that I knew everything was all right.' The bride promised to obey her new husband, and the couple left the Abbey to the strains of Mendelssohn's 'Wedding March'.

This was the first time newsreel cameras had been allowed to follow a wedding party into the Abbey itself – an omen, perhaps, of the modernizing role Prince Philip would come to play within the Royal Family. Crowds around the world rushed to the cinemas to watch the film. In occupied Berlin, a four-thousand-seater cinema was packed day after day.

The royal couple were pictured at Buckingham Palace after the wedding ceremony. Designer Norman Hartnell took inspiration from Botticelli's paintings for the bride's dress, and the embroidery of flowers was picked out in crystal and some 10,000 pearls.

New Elizabethans

The early years of the marriage were eased by the fact that Elizabeth had not yet acceded to the throne. Philip, she wrote to her mother from honeymoon, 'is terribly independent and I quite understand the poor darling wanting to start off properly, without everything being done for us.' Philip for his part wrote to his new mother-in-law: 'Cherish Lilibet? I wonder if that word is enough to express what is in me?' He had earlier told his future mother-in-law that he had fallen in love 'completely and unreservedly'.

Theirs was at this point a two-career marriage. Philip set off each morning to walk to his job at the Admiralty. Elizabeth was asked to perform an increasing number of public engagements – the royal wedding had made her even more interesting in the public's eyes – but her most immediate ambition now lay elsewhere.

On 4 June 1948, the Palace announced that the twenty-two-year-old Princess was expecting a child, and the public became obsessed with the impending arrival. Meanwhile, the young couple were (to Philip's relief) planning to move out of Buckingham Palace, and the shadow of Elizabeth's parents, and into a home of their own the King had offered them. Clarence House was in a poor state of repair but Philip delightedly took charge of the renovations, while the cumbersome machinery surrounding the birth of the next heir to the throne swung into place.

The King issued Letters Patent to ensure that the baby would bear the title prince or princess, not normally accorded to the offspring of a king's female descendant. And it was decided, for the first time, to dispense with the archaic tradition that the Home Secretary should be present at such an important birth. Objections, predictably, came from that arch-conservative the Queen, but gave way when it was pointed out that all the countries of which the baby might one day be sovereign could ask to send their own representatives, and the corridor outside the birthing room might get a little crowded . . .

On 14 November, Prince Charles was born, in Princess Elizabeth's own bedroom, with four doctors in attendance and all the facilities of a hospital suite installed nearby. Prince Philip was summoned from the Palace squash courts, and the fountains in Trafalgar Square flowed blue for a boy. The baby was placed in a gilt crib and displayed to the waiting courtiers. One remarked, on hearing the baby was a boy, that he'd known Princess Elizabeth wouldn't let them down.

On 15 December, the baby was christened in the Buckingham Palace Music Room with the names Charles Philip Arthur George. The Princess at first fed her son herself, but motherhood did not impede what must, in retrospect, have been the most carefree period of her life. She celebrated her twenty-third birthday at the Café de Paris, with Laurence Olivier and Vivien Leigh in the company.

A few months later she and Philip finally moved into Clarence House – but only briefly. In October Philip was appointed First Lieutenant of HMS *Chequers*, of the Royal Navy's Mediterranean Fleet based in Malta. He flew out there immediately and Princess Elizabeth soon joined him, leaving baby Charles behind.

Cecil Beaton, photographing Princess Elizabeth with her four-week-old son, recalled that baby Charles was 'an obedient sitter'. Elizabeth's flower basket brooch was given by her parents to celebrate the birth of their first grandchild.

The first four years of marriage gave the royal couple a taste of normal life. While Prince Philip was stationed in Malta, Elizabeth accompanied him to Rome to watch him playing with the Malta Naval Polo Team in April 1951.

The pattern of her life over the next year or so would be of lengthy visits to Malta interspersed with periods at home. Her time in Malta as a Navy wife was the closest to a normal (albeit a privileged) life Elizabeth would ever know. The Edinburghs, as they were known, were living in a villa belonging to Philip's uncle Lord Mountbatten, a commander of the Mediterranean Fleet. From there Elizabeth could drive around the island in her Daimler, swim off the beach, visit the hairdresser, dine at the local hotel.

On 15 August 1950, at Clarence House, she gave birth to another baby, Princess Anne; and ill health forced her to stay in the UK for some months before once again flying back to Malta to spend Christmas with her husband, who was that year promoted to command of the HMS *Magpie*. The couple were able also to enjoy a visit to Philip's native Greece – but their days of pleasure were soon curtailed.

George VI's health had been steadily deteriorating, and his haggard appearance when he opened the Festival of Britain in May 1951 marked a visible downturn. That summer exploratory surgery revealed that the King was suffering from lung cancer. It was expected that Princess Elizabeth would have to take on more of his duties – and expected she would do so with her husband at her side. Prince Philip's promising naval career had come to an early end.

In October 1951, when the couple set off for a tour of Canada and the United States, the King's state of health was such that Elizabeth's private secretary slept with the documents necessary to confirm her accession to the throne under his bed. The visit saw complaints in the Canadian press that Elizabeth seemed never to be smiling. To appear always serious and dignified in public was in fact a lesson her grandmother

The royal couple were in Kenya in February when Elizabeth learnt of her accession to the throne. Here they are in the gardens of Sagana Lodge, presented to them as a wedding gift from the people of Kenya.

The new Queen reviews the Grenadier Guards on the occasion of her 26th birthday, less than three months after her father's death.

Queen Mary had taught her, but Philip tried not only to relieve the strain of the tour but to encourage her to show a more approachable face.

When they moved on to America, however, it marked the start of Elizabeth's long love affair with that nation. It certainly seemed safe for the Princess to represent her father on an even more ambitious foreign trip. Though King George seemed to rally over Christmas at Sandringham with his family, there could be no question of his undertaking the long-planned six-month tour of the rest of the Commonwealth.

Elizabeth and Philip would go instead – with the treat, before the tour proper began, of a short stay in Kenya, at the safari lodge that had been given to them as a wedding present. They could also spend a night at Treetops, just 10 miles away – the hotel in the branches of a giant fig tree.

On 31 January 1952 the King stood on the tarmac at London airport to wave goodbye to his daughter. They would never see each other again.

Princess Victoria, roused from sleep, had been wearing a dressing gown when she heard the news that she was queen; Elizabeth was in safari kit, fresh down from a night game viewing from the platform at Treetops. She was probably one of the last world figures to hear the news that had already been broadcast all over the globe: that George VI had died suddenly, in his sleep. On 5 February he had been out shooting at Sandringham; on the morning of the 6th, his valet found him dead.

In remote Kenya, it was a journalist who told Elizabeth's private secretary, who told Prince Philip's equerry, Mike Parker. Parker told Prince Philip, who looked 'as if you'd dropped half the world on him'. It was for Philip to tell Elizabeth – or, as she now was, the Queen. He took her out into the garden and observers saw them walking up and down together, 'talking, talking, talking'.

Personal grief must have been her first and overwhelming emotion – not a given for royal heirs in British history. But when she went back into the Kenyan safari lodge and her lady-in-waiting, Pamela Mountbatten, offered sympathy, Elizabeth responded with an apology. 'I'm so sorry, it means we're all going to have to go back home.' There were telegrams and documents even before she returned to Entebbe and began the twenty-four-hour flight to the UK.

When, at dusk on 7 February, she landed at London airport to be greeted by her ministers on the tarmac, she was composed, even managing a faint smile of thanks for their homage. But her secretary saw she had been crying, privately. Among those waiting was her Prime Minister, Winston Churchill, and it was he who set the tone for the new reign. 'Famous have been the reigns of our Queens,' he declared.

She drove to Clarence House – where, half an hour later, Queen Mary arrived to kiss her granddaughter's hand. It must have brought Elizabeth's new position shockingly home. The next morning she walked to St James's Palace for the Accession Council.

She read her declaration of sovereignty. 'My heart is too full for me to say more today, than that I shall always work as my father did throughout his reign, to uphold the constitutional government, and to advance the happiness and prosperity of my peoples . . . I pray that God will help me discharge worthily this heavy task that has been laid on me so early in my life.'

Her father was not yet buried. The bringing back of his body from Sandringham for a London lying in state before burial at Windsor, saw not only extraordinary scenes of public grief but the iconic image of three queens in mourning: his mother, Queen Mary; his widow, Queen Elizabeth (now to be called Queen Elizabeth the Queen Mother); and the new Queen Elizabeth II. It would be another sixteen months before Elizabeth II was crowned – but already the new reign was underway.

The first few months, and the first few years, of the Queen's reign gave some very specific indications – both for better and for worse – of what lay ahead.

From the start, the precedents were invoked of Elizabeth I, and of Victoria. The Queen herself dismissed comparisons with the first Elizabeth, a woman who did not enjoy her own blessings of husband and family, and who ruled in an age before constitutional monarchy. But it was perhaps telling that Elizabeth II would open her first Parliament wearing Queen Victoria's crown. The long reign of Elizabeth's great-great-grandmother had seen the monarchy through some testing times.

Now, however, the huge public optimism centred around the idea of a New Elizabethan Age. The coronation, said Princess Margaret later, was like 'a phoenix-time', when the world seemed reborn from the ashes of the War. All the more so when, on Coronation Day itself, came news that a British-led party had at last attained the summit of Mount Everest.

In Elizabeth's immediate family circle, however, the mood was not so happy. By now in her mid-eighties, Queen Mary was becoming increasingly frail. But the Queen's mother and sister also felt themselves cut adrift. Her mother was reluctant to move out of Buckingham Palace – almost as reluctant as Elizabeth's husband was to move in.

Prince Philip had been thrown into gloom by the change in his and his wife's circumstances – and it was not necessarily only the courtiers who made him feel excluded. Elizabeth's determination to get to grips with her duties caused her to keep influence and information strictly in her own hands.

Recalling the period, Prince Philip said that before the Queen's accession whatever they did was done together, and 'I suppose I naturally filled the principal position. In 1952 the whole thing changed, very considerably.'

The Queen did announce that her husband was to have 'place, pre-eminence and precedence' after her 'on all occasions and in all meetings, except where otherwise provided by Act of Parliament'. She also ended the custom whereby the sovereign's spouse had to bow or curtsy when the sovereign entered a room. But such gestures could only go so far. In public, Prince Philip must always call the Queen 'Ma'am'. (Small wonder if, in private, he sometimes speaks to her with a brusque frankness that is his way of letting off steam.)

There had always been debate about the role of a male consort, and his precise place in the royal pecking order. A king's wife, after all, would not expect to be privy to the red boxes of state papers, or present at the weekly audiences with Prime Ministers. Why should it be any different for a queen's husband?

One issue did relate specifically to Philip's masculinity – the question of a surname. Shortly after Elizabeth's accession, it was reported to a furious Queen Mary that Philip's Uncle Louis had been heard boasting at a dinner party. The House of Mountbatten, he claimed, now sat on the throne. When the Queen, strongly urged by her ministers, announced that her descendants would keep the name of Windsor, Philip was deeply wounded. He was, he said, 'just a bloody amoeba' – the only man in the country not allowed to give his children his name.

Meanwhile, the Queen's difficulties in juggling duty with family was visible in other ways. Three months before the coronation, old Queen Mary died. Then, at the ceremony itself, Princess Margaret was observed picking a piece of fluff off the lapel of Group Captain Peter Townsend – a tiny gesture intimate enough to alert press and public to a romance of which Margaret's family was already only too aware.

PICTURE
POST

Vol. 59, No. 11
13 June, 1953

I/-
Special
Coronation Souvenir
Number

God Save the Queen

Newspapers and magazines around the world were full of the glamorous new young Queen, and of her Coronation.

The marriage of such a close member of her family required the Queen's consent. Townsend was a war hero, admired and trusted by the Royal Family. But he was also a divorced man, at a time when divorce was still a huge social barrier. The shadow of Edward VIII and Mrs Simpson loomed large. More importantly, the Queen (who shared her mother's sincere and traditional Christian faith) was Supreme Governor of a Church of England which did not sanction remarriage after divorce.

Princess Margaret believed that when she turned twenty-five, in two years' time, she might be able to marry Peter Townsend without the Queen's official sanction and still keep her place in the Royal Family. But when that time came in 1955, she found instead that she would have to relinquish all royal rights and privileges. 'Mindful of the Church's teachings,' she decided, as she famously declared, 'not to marry Group Captain Townsend.' But perhaps the Townsend affair had revealed Elizabeth's tendency to avoid dealing with emotional problems – and revealed, too, the refusal to put any family claim ahead of what she saw as her duty which was being displayed in several other ways.

The six-month, thirteen-country, 40,000-mile Commonwealth tour on which the Queen and Prince Philip embarked in November 1953 was a vital affirmation of the Queen's personal and enduring belief in the value of the Commonwealth. The organization which gives her a link to some third of the world's population seemed particularly important at a moment when nations once part of the British Empire, were claiming their independence one by one.

The trip was an immense success. In New Zealand, the UK High Commissioner reported that 'Few, I think, could have predicted the adulation which Her Majesty and His Royal Highness . . . inspired wherever they went, or indeed the emotions which Her Majesty's presence aroused . . . no longer is she a remote personage to her New Zealand peoples: she is now, to them, the Queen of New Zealand.' It had, he said, brought the reality of the Commonwealth home to them in a manner 'which no amount of writing or talking could ever have accomplished'.

But the enduring memory of the tour now is not of the Queen in Jamaica or in Tonga, Sri Lanka or Australia, in any one of the hundred outfits Norman Hartnell had designed for the 'world's sweetheart'. It is of the return home, in May 1954, when she met her children again, after months apart – and said 'No, not you, dear', to her five-year-old son, greeting dignitaries first before shaking Charles's hand.

Princess Anne, many years later, would speak to the journalist and author Andrew Marr of having enjoyed 'pretty good mothering'. It was a mothering exercised within a strict timetable, but that might apply to a 'Service' family. The fact was, Elizabeth could no longer be primarily a mother, or a sister, or a wife. She was first and foremost the Queen.

One chain of crises with which she had to deal in these early years was not personal in nature but constitutional. But perhaps they are as revealing of the Queen's personality. Winston Churchill was her first Prime Minister, and one who learned to respect her as much as she did him. However, Winston Churchill's health was

Four generations of the Royal Family. After the christening of her daughter Princess Anne on 21 October 1950, the Queen was photographed with her mother and her grandmother Queen Mary.

failing – though the young Queen Elizabeth II was understandably reluctant to play any part in forcing the great statesman to retire.

Churchill was succeeded in office by Anthony Eden in April 1955, but in the latter part of 1956 the Suez Crisis brought about Eden's downfall. Britain had made a covert alliance with France and Israel to seize back from Egypt control of the Suez Canal. There are enduring questions as to just what the Queen did or did not know about this armed aggression towards a country with which Britain was not at war.

On Eden's resignation it devolved on the Queen to invite another politician to head the Conservative Party, and to form a government. Her invitation to Harold Macmillan (rather than to the other contender, Rab Butler) was based on leading Conservative opinion – but it was seen as showing her in thrall to a limited circle of Tory grandees. Six years later the situation would be repeated when Macmillan tried to ensure that he himself would be succeeded not by Butler, but by the aristocratic Alec Douglas-Home.

One way and another the questions that arose out of the early years of the Queen's reign were those that would dog her through the next decades.

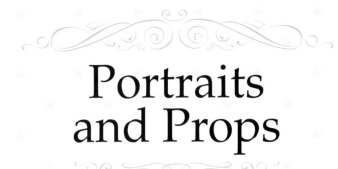

Portraits and Props

Not long into the new reign the Italian portrait painter, Pietro Annigoni, was commissioned by a City of London livery company to paint a portrait of the Queen. It has become one of the images that define her early reign. A figure at once restrained and romanticized, she is seen in the robes of the Order of the Garter, against a faded sylvan landscape, gazing out at something the viewer cannot see. Annigoni said it was inspired by a very human story the Queen told him, of how as a child she had loved to gaze out of the window at the people below. Some complained, nonetheless, that Annigoni had painted an icon of monarchy, rather than a living monarch – but the Queen herself is known to have liked a work that the public stood ten deep to see.

Well over a hundred artists have painted the Queen – usually to commission and from life, though the image Andy Warhol made of her in 1985 was one famous exception. And we all handle portraits of the Queen every day. They jingle in our pockets on coins and send our letters on their way; through the Commonwealth as well as in Britain. The postage stamps alone are said to make hers the most reproduced portrait in history.

Her image on coins, like that on banknotes, has been updated over the years, and she is surely realistic about seeing herself age – a woman comparatively without vanity. In 2001, famously or infamously, Lucian Freud painted the Queen and the result was unpopular with many, since it showed her looking lowering, lined and lumpy. But in fact painter and sitter had got on well, bonding over a shared interest in horses.

Photographic portraits have been many, but a few stand out. Cecil Beaton photographed the Queen repeatedly in her younger years. 'I was always impressed by, and grateful for, the exceptionally charming manners that the young princesses had in relation to the job of being photographed,' he wrote. 'Unlike other children, royal or otherwise, by whom I have been victimized, they never showed signs of restlessness.'

Later, Beaton photographed Princess Elizabeth in ATS uniform and as a young mother; would take the first photographs of Prince Charles, and of Princess Anne ('an infant version of the Sleeping Beauty', Beaton called the latter image, as Prince Charles kissed his sister on the cheek). He also, of course, took the stunning image of the Queen on her Coronation Day: composed, regal and beautiful with her crown, sceptre and orb, against a ghostly background of Westminster Abbey.

Dorothy Wilding had taken early black-and-white photographs of the Queen; Eve Arnold took her in 1968 with a black umbrella and a broad smile. Patrick Lichfield snapped her in 1971 laughing down from the deck of the Royal Yacht *Britannia* and in 1978 Lord Snowdon took a portrait of her holding her first grandson. A quarter of a century later, in 2004, Chris Levine's holographic portrait unusually showed her with eyes closed, as he asked her to relax between the eight-second shots.

It was Jane Bown, herself an octogenarian, who took the official portrait of the Queen for her eightieth birthday. Soon after came the notable series of portraits Annie Leibovitz took in 2007, in advance of the Queen's first official visit to the USA for sixteen years.

The two did not get on easily. Leibovitz arrived with an entourage, expecting far more time than the Queen was able to give, and suggested the monarch remove her 'crown' (actually a tiara) to look less 'dressy'. The Queen praised by contrast the low-key style of Jane Bown, who with the monarch herself had shifted furniture around the room as necessary.

But in the end the Queen came through, as she always does. Leibovitz was able to photograph her both with and without her Garter robes, in images that consciously reflect the richness of paintings on the palace walls. And Annie Leibovitz would be invited back to take another series of remarkable images – this time, to mark the Queen's ninetieth birthday.

It is often said that the Queen is uninterested in clothes. This is not altogether true – but it is true that for her the sheer appeal of a garment can never be paramount. She is – said one of her favourite designers, Hardy Amies – wary of clothes that are 'too chic'. 'The Queen's attitude is that she must always be dressed for the occasion.'

Very often, of course, that means a lavish evening dress with elbow-length gloves and a blaze of jewellery. Relaxing at Balmoral, it may mean woollens and stout brogues, or jodhpurs and tweed jacket. Certain ceremonies require the Queen to wear uniform, and she has always been particular about correct detail and fit. Riding sidesaddle to take the salute at the Trooping of the Colour, she used to wear the uniform of the regiment whose colours were being trooped, adjusting her diet if necessary in the weeks beforehand to fit the exiguous tight jacket and full skirt.

In her youth the Queen cut a glamorous figure, her enviably slim and petite figure honed and fit from her hours of riding. In the heady post-war days of Christian Dior's New Look the two princesses, Elizabeth and Margaret, had been given a private view of his fabulous full-skirted creations, though in an age of rationing and austerity they could never be allowed to wear them. Instead, Elizabeth turned to the romantic but restrained designs of noted (and safely British) designer Norman Hartnell, already her mother's favourite.

The outfits worn by the Princess Elizabeth as a child were copied around the globe. Her mother's choice of colour for her daughter made yellow the fashion for little girls everywhere. But Hartnell said once that the adult Elizabeth had no desire to be a fashion setter. 'That's left for other people with less important work to do.'

All the same, with the help of Hartnell, and later Hardy Amies, she had a fashionable youth – followed, perhaps, by a less stylish middle age. She reached midlife in the 1960s, just as the clothes of the young began to deviate more sharply than at any time in history from those their parents wore. And though Princess Margaret, relaxing in Mustique, might allow herself to be photographed in flowing kaftans, that would never do for the Queen.

She suffered, too, from allowing herself still to be guided by the old-fashioned advice of her one-time nursemaid Bobo MacDonald, who became her dresser . . . and perhaps from a figure which, however suited to 1950s styles, did not lend itself to the high fashion of later years. Ironically, it is in old age that the Queen has once more come into her own as an extremely glamorous (great-)granny, aided by the advice and designs of Angela Kelly, who since 2002 has perhaps come as close as anyone could do to taking Bobo's place.

In youth or age, however, there are rules to royal dressing which the Queen – ever comfortable with regulations and ceremonials – feels no desire to break. Colours must be light or bright, so as to show up from a distance (the same reason the Queen always wears bright lipstick). Hats – and she is said to have worn some five thousand of them – must be made so as not to hide the face. Hemlines must not be too short, and hems must be weighted where necessary to avoid embarrassing wardrobe malfunctions. Angela Kelly described how the ever-practical Queen urged her to crumple any fabric she planned to use, to see how badly it creased.

Annigoni's portrait, entitled 'Queen Elizabeth II, Queen Regent' soon became one of the iconic images of the new sovereign.

In so far as they are designed for public appearance and for photographs, some of the Queen's day dresses may be made surprisingly plain. They are after all only backdrops for the jewellery she calls her 'best bits' – and for the hats, the gloves, the famous boxy handbags. (Designers rail against those handbags, and even against the jewels which outshine the actual garments – but the Queen knows what it is the public wants to see.)

On tours abroad, the Queen's dress must conform to the customs of the host nation, so that a visit to the Middle East may see her covered from chin to heel, even in the heat of day. Or it may compliment that country – the Queen wore green for a groundbreaking visit to Ireland, and at Balmoral, in tribute to their Scottish blood, members of the Royal Family often appear in tartan. In a sense, all the Queen's garments are a uniform – the bright hats and dresses as much as the regimentals. They are equipment – props – which help the Queen perform the job in hand, whatever that might be.

Part II
Being Queen
1956–1986

(Clockwise from top) The Queen and Prince Philip with
their two eldest children; the wedding of Prince Charles
and Lady Diana Spencer; the Queen wearing the robes
of the Order of the Garter.

Work and Family

The single most important moments of the Queen's working day take place away from the public gaze. The battered red or blue leather dispatch boxes of state papers are delivered to her daily, wherever she may be, and 'Reader No. I' studies them religiously. The 1969 documentary film Royal Family even showed them being lowered from a helicopter on to the deck of Britannia. Lead-lined and bombproof, these are boxes to which only she and her private secretaries have a key.

The formidable amount of information they contain is supplemented by that gleaned from audiences given to ministers, officers, senior clergy, and by meetings with foreign envoys. (Ambassadors newly appointed to the UK have still to present their credentials to the Queen.) That is why successive British Prime Ministers – and Theresa May is the Queen's thirteenth – have found their weekly meetings with her so useful, and why Commonwealth Prime Ministers express the same feelings. By now, there is quite literally no one who can offer a broader panorama of experience, particularly when it comes to foreign affairs, no one who has met more leading figures of the past century.

Not that she would use her experience or her position to impose her views. On the tiny handful of occasions when the Queen has even hinted at an opinion on a political matter, it has been headline news. She has the constitutional right to be consulted, to encourage, and to warn. But this Queen (or so we believe, for her conversations with the Prime Minister are wholly private) draws back from offering advice. Her way of asking a telling question, however, can cause a minister to think twice.

Alongside the state-level communications, the Queen has always tried to read as many as possible of the letters she receives from the public, which she sees as being 'rather personal to oneself' – and also a good clue as to what people are thinking. She also, of course, engages more directly with the public on her huge tally of royal engagements – though interestingly, the 'walkabouts' we now think of as an integral part of those duties began only in 1970. Her engagements today are fewer (and shorter) than they once were, but in 2015, the year before her ninetieth birthday, she still carried out 306 engagements in the UK, and 35 abroad.

Openings and inspections; anniversaries of organizations of which she is patron; hospitals, exhibitions and factories. Some events are glamorous – in 1956 she famously met Marilyn Monroe at a film premiere – others better described as worthy. But it is part of her job to take all her engagements seriously. That very seriousness was itself something of an issue in early days. Both her husband and her ministers wished that she would learn to smile more readily, but in the early part of her reign, at least, she believed what people wanted from her was solemnity.

British royalty and Hollywood royalty often meet. In 1956 the Queen shook hands with Marilyn Monroe at a premiere of *The Battle of the River Plate*.

Some six years into her reign, the Queen is pictured as a working woman, at her desk in Buckingham Palace with the red box of state papers she receives every day.

Many of the Queen's speeches are written by her private secretaries, though she then reviews and edits the draft, in consultation with Prince Philip. Most personal to her are the Christmas broadcasts she makes every year. Her delivery has changed over the years, and her accent is less formidably aristocratic than it used to be. However, her public speaking is something for which she was once criticized. In 1957, the rebellious peer and magazine editor John Grigg, Baron Altrincham, wrote an article in which he complained that the Queen's speeches reflected her own lack of proper training and the stick-in-the-muds around her.

'The personality conveyed by the utterances which are put into her mouth is that of a priggish schoolgirl,' Altrincham wrote. Altrincham was perceptive in his suggestion that the Queen was faced with the 'seemingly impossible task of being at once ordinary and extraordinary'. But he was hit with a storm of criticism – he even had his faced slapped in the street. Such was the atmosphere of the 1950s.

His was not the only critical voice. In the same year, the journalist and broadcaster Malcolm Muggeridge wrote that the monarchy needed some new advisers if they wanted to prevent themselves and their lives from becoming 'a sort of royal soap opera'. The Queen had to cease being merely 'a generator of snobbishness and a focus of sycophancy'.

Coincidentally or otherwise, the last of the 'presentation parties' by which aristocratic debutantes were presented at court took place the following year. But the Queen's life was and is still marked out by other, more significant ceremonies.

Some annual fixtures are comparatively modern. Others bear the weight of history. Among the former are the annual garden parties, each for some eight thousand guests, selected for their public service, and drinking some twenty-seven thousand cups of tea in the grounds of Buckingham Palace or Holyroodhouse. The Queen and other members of the Royal Family pass through lanes between the guests, a few of whom are singled out for presentation by the top-hatted Gentleman Ushers. Another nineteenth-century institution was the Royal Command Performance – the most famous of them today is the annual all-star charity event, now known as the Royal Variety Performance. Over the years the Queen has witnessed and met performers from George Formby to Noël Coward, and Count Basie to Lady Gaga.

The Queen learned to ride sidesaddle especially for the annual ceremony of Trooping the Colour. It is one of the most impressive fixtures in her calendar – even in the pouring rain!

Trooping the Colour – or the Sovereign's Birthday Parade – takes place in June, the month of the Queen's official birthday. The Household Cavalry and the five regiments of the Guards Division salute the sovereign and troop their 'colour' or regimental standard. For many years now the ceremony has been followed by a flypast of RAF planes over Buckingham Palace.

The Queen is what is known as the Fountain of Honour in the United Kingdom – the only one with the right to confer honours on her subjects. Some twenty-four investiture ceremonies are held each year at Buckingham Palace and every five years, one at the Palace of Holyroodhouse, where the Queen herself or a senior member of the Royal Family pins the decoration on each person mentioned in the New Year's and Birthday Honours Lists. Or, in the case of those receiving a knighthood, 'dubs' him on the shoulder with her father's sword.

The greatest honour of all is to become a Knight Companion of the Most Noble Order of the Garter, founded in 1348, membership of which (apart from the sovereign and the heir to the throne) is restricted to twenty-four knights or ladies at any one time. Each June sees a procession of the Garter Knights at Windsor, led by the Queen and Prince Philip in the Order's dark blue mantle – lined with white taffeta, and with a flash of red hood on the right shoulder – and Tudor bonnet with huge white plume. The blue Garter itself, worn by men on

Each year Windsor sees the procession of the Knights and Ladies of the Order of the Garter. Admission to this ancient and exclusive order is the Queen's personal gift.

the left knee and women on the left arm, bears the famous legend 'Honi soit qui mal y pense'. Shame on he who evil thinks.

Also dating back to medieval times (though it had lapsed, and was revived only in the 1930s) is a rite that takes place on Maundy Thursday, three days before Easter, and recalls Jesus washing the feet of his disciples. Until the seventeenth century, in a ritual gesture of humility monarchs actually washed the feet of a number of poor people, one for every year of the sovereign's own age. Today's Queen merely distributes 'Maundy money' – specially minted coins borne on trays by the beruffed Yeomen of the Guard – to elderly persons notable for work in their community. On Remembrance Sunday, the second Sunday in November, the Queen appears in mourning black, a colour she would not normally wear, at the Cenotaph in Whitehall to honour the war dead of all the Commonwealth nations.

Each autumn, and the aftermath of a general election, sees the State Opening of Parliament. The Queen, with the Imperial State Crown travelling in a separate carriage before her, drives to the Palace of Westminster. There, preceded by the Sword of State and the Cap of Maintenance, she progresses through to the House of Lords wearing her crown and long-trained crimson Parliamentary Robe.

An arcane piece of ritual sees the official known as Black Rod go to summon the Commons, only to have the door slammed in his face, in token of the House of Commons's independence. The Prime Minister and Leader of the Opposition are then led into the Lords to hear the annual Queen's Speech (which in fact is written for her by her government), setting out plans for the coming Session. Since there have been moments in the nation's history at which the Crown might well have regarded Parliament as enemy territory, a 'hostage' MP spends the duration of the royal visit at Buckingham Palace as guarantee of the monarch's safe return.

Prince Philip has always accompanied the Queen to the State Opening and they walk together through the Houses of Parliament, her hand resting on his, both their hands held aloft. But his seat on the dais, to the left of her throne, is a little lower than hers. He has no official ceremonial role, nor has he access to those red boxes of state papers. It has always been an exceptionally difficult position for a man who – by background, temperament and generation – would in other circumstances have expected not only to have his own successful career, but to be the unquestioned head of his family.

The State Opening of Parliament has always seen the Queen enthroned in the House of Lords wearing the Imperial State Crown in full ceremonial regalia. It was announced that 2017's State Opening would break with tradition and be a 'dressed down' ceremony.

Just as the first adjustments of the new reign were over and everyone was settling in for the long haul, there had been rumours of trouble between the Queen and her husband. In the autumn of 1956 Prince Philip, with his wife's blessing, set out on a four-month solo tour of the Commonwealth – time back at sea, aboard the Royal Yacht *Britannia*, but perhaps also time away from the constraints of his new life.

But the trip took a sour turn when one of his travelling companions, Mike Parker, was summoned home to answer charges of adultery in the divorce courts. Gleeful press speculation inevitably turned to Philip himself, and particularly his regular attendance at an all-male luncheon club, the Thursday Club. It was a raffish group, beset with rumours of ribaldry and 'party girls'. The Queen's press secretary, most unusually, issued a statement: 'It is quite untrue that there is any rift between the Queen and the Duke.'

Philip's solo journey ended in February 1957 when his wife joined him in Portugal. In her Christmas message the Queen had told the world that of all the voices she had heard that day, none had given her greater pleasure than her husband's. She had just created him a Prince of the United Kingdom – a higher rank than the dukedom he had held since their marriage.

Though his position continued to chafe him, as he walked two paces behind his wife, he found a productive way to accommodate himself to the situation. Patronage of some 850 organizations (more even than are sponsored by the Queen); a particular interest in science and technology; an early sponsorship of the Outward Bound scheme; and, from 1956, the Duke of Edinburgh's Award to recognize young people's achievement in pursuing the ideals he himself learned at Gordonstoun, of a healthy mind in a healthy body. The scheme – now expanded around the globe – has helped some eight million young people since its foundation. He also took over management of the family's estates.

Prince Philip has always displayed a concern for bringing the monarchy more in tune with the modern era. He has often been a force for change, insisting on the reform of some of the more arcane practices of the Royal Household, like the powdering of footman's wigs.

His list of engagements always rivalled his wife's, and he has always cheered and encouraged the Queen into what she did not at first find easy – the social,

This picture from 1951 shows the Queen (then Princess Elizabeth) with her husband and two eldest children as a new family group of 'we four'.

(top) The Queen at the wheel of a Daimler with Prince Charles and Princess Anne as passengers.
(bottom) The Queen has always been a keen photographer. At the Windsor Horse Show in 1982 she captured her husband Philip with a Leica camera.

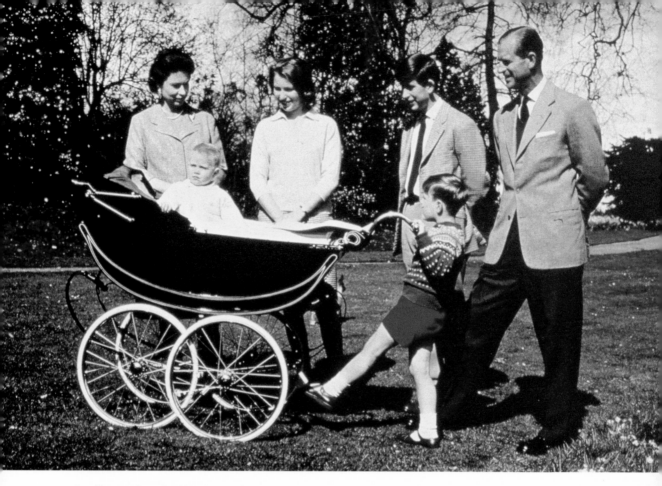

Four become six . . . By 1965, when the family celebrated the Queen's 39th birthday at Windsor, Princes Andrew and Edward had made the family group complete.

crowd-pleasing aspect of her duties. He is, said his grandson Prince William, 'always on her [the Queen's] side, and he's an unwavering companion.' One who 'totally put his personal career aside to support her, and he never takes the limelight, never oversteps the mark.' But of course that is not the only side of the story.

Perhaps the Duke's famous gaffes, his brusqueness with the press and the impatience he has shown privately even to his wife are an essential escape valve – a letting off of steam. They may be just the natural expression of a man of his age and background – or even a cheerful playing to the gallery. ('Often naughty, never nasty,' wrote Kurt Hahn, the founder of Gordonstoun, about Philip, prophetically.). But Philip is a man not temperamentally attuned to life in his wife's shadow, and claims that he sought consolation elsewhere have never gone away.

The Queen's own way of ameliorating the difficulties was to allow her husband to wear the trousers in their private life. But that decision in itself had consequences. It was at Philip's urging that Prince Charles was sent to school, rather than being

In the early days of their marriage, Elizabeth and Philip were able to relax with their baby son Charles at Windlesham Moor, the Victorian house they rented in Surrey.

educated at home – later, more specifically, to Gordonstoun, whose bracing atmosphere had suited Philip himself but which his eldest son found desperately uncongenial.

The questions surrounding Philip and his role were the same as had been raised about Prince Albert more than a century before. Then it was Victoria herself who sought to limit Albert's actual role, as opposed to his ceremonial rank and precedence, to what she called 'help with the blotting paper'. However, over the years his would prove a beneficial and a calming influence: one which, in his insistence that the Crown should be above party politics, and Victoria no longer indulge her personal prejudices and favourites, set the path for the modern monarchy.

What gave Albert his opportunity to play a larger part in state affairs were Victoria's pregnancies – her 'plagues' – as she called them. With his wife quite literally confined by five children in six years, with four more to follow, Albert became, as he hoped, not only 'the natural head of the family' but Victoria's 'sole confidential adviser in politics . . . her private secretary and her permanent Minister'. No one, of course, could foresee Albert's early death and its effect on Victoria . . . Elizabeth was luckier in a notably long-lasting marriage which overcame any early difficulties. By the end of the 1950s Elizabeth was anxious to have more children. In the summer of 1959, after a long wait, she found she was pregnant at last. Prince Andrew was born on 19 February 1960, Prince Edward would follow on 10 March 1964. And before Andrew's birth the Queen was able to make one concession at least to her husband's feelings. As her Prime Minister Harold Macmillan wrote in his diary: 'The Queen only wishes (properly enough) to do something to please her husband – with whom she is desperately in love.'

While the Royal Family as such would continue to be described as the House of Windsor, those descendants of the Queen who were not designated a royal highness would be Mountbatten-Windsors. It was, she said, when she announced the plan, 'close to her heart'.

Within hours of each birth, Queen Elizabeth – no Victoria – was asking to see official papers. All the same, her relationship with her second pair of children, so much younger than the first, was considerably more 'hands-on' – helped by her own increased confidence, her ability to fulfil her royal role without allowing it to consume her.

She would often bathe and put Andrew and Edward to bed, would allow them to race their bikes along the Windsor corridors, indulging them perhaps all the more for the fact that she had seen less of her elder children, now away at boarding school. The younger sons would feel less acutely than their elder siblings the fact that their mother was determined above all to do her public duty – was in effect the most notable career woman in her country.

The Queen here delightedly encourages her sons as Prince Charles treats his youngest brother Edward to a go-kart ride.

Changing Faces

The 1960s had started on a bright note for the Royal Family, with the wedding of Princess Margaret – though her marriage to a commoner, Tony Armstrong-Jones, was controversial for the day. Macmillan remembered how, arriving at Windsor, he was greeted by the Queen's uncle the Duke of Gloucester with the words: 'Thank goodness you've come, Prime Minister. The Queen is in a terrible state. There's a man called Jones in the library who says he wants to marry her sister.' But in the end, of course, she gave her consent.

It is possible that, after the Peter Townsend debacle, she simply could not bear once again to thwart her sister – whose flamboyant career as an unmarried woman in London's smart set was itself becoming the subject of critical comment. In the event the marriage of the fairy-tale princess to the charming and glamorous photographer gave a welcome note of modernity to the Royal Family.

On 6 May 1960, a hundred thousand people crowded the streets to watch the bride drive to Westminster Abbey, in a dress designed by Hartnell to the groom's instructions. Tony Armstrong-Jones initially refused the title offered to him by the Queen, but before the couple's first child was born in November 1961, he consented to become the Earl of Snowdon.

In the second decade of the Queen's reign, in an era of unprecedented change, the initial enthusiasm that had greeted the New Elizabethan Age in the 1950s was beginning to die away. The monarchy could no longer rely on unquestioning support. As early as 1963, the BBC's new satirical show *That Was the Week That Was* could perform a spoof of the royal barge sinking with the Royal Family on board.

It is true that one potential problem for the monarchy had simply melted away. A succession of Conservative and essentially aristocratic Prime Ministers – with power passed from Churchill to Eden, and then from Macmillan to Alec Douglas-Home – had first been broken when the Labour victory of 1964 brought Yorkshireman

Harold Wilson into power. Palace officials were taken aback when Wilson arrived to kiss hands not only accompanied by a large group of his family, but wearing a strange variant of the traditional formal morning dress.

The Queen put Wilson on his toes by quizzing him on the country's financial problems, about which, he said, she was better informed than he, and leaving him feeling 'like an unprepared schoolboy'. Within weeks 'he would have died for her', a lady-in-waiting reported. It was during Wilson's first year in office that the Queen had to read the secret protocols arranging the government of Britain in the event of a nuclear attack. These were, after all, the years of the Cold War.

A foreshadow of the events of the late 1990s came in 1966 when an avalanche of mud and debris cascaded on to the Welsh mining village of Aberfan, engulfing its primary school, killing more than a hundred children. The Queen, urged to go there immediately, refused, and for the best of motives. The arrangements for her visit

As Queen of the United Kingdom, Elizabeth II addressed the Council of Europe, an international human rights organization, in the Banqueting House at Whitehall in May 1969.

might distract from the rescue effort – what if she caused rescuers to miss 'some poor child that might have been found under the wreckage?' she asked. When she did visit a week later, her emotion was palpable; sorry, as she told the villagers with tears in her eyes, 'I can give you nothing except sympathy.' But in the years ahead such restraint could be misunderstood, and taken for a lack of care.

By the end of the 1960s, polls were finding more people who thought the monarchy an out-of-touch anachronism – and, in a youth-oriented era, hailing the idea that the heir to the throne should automatically succeed when he or she reached thirty-five. Some polls found the Queen merely 'not unpopular' in the country. There was (with inflation making the royal finances less secure) an increasing awareness of a need to sell the monarchy to the people – a 'distinct wind of change at the Palace', as a BBC memo put it. The royals reacted surprisingly readily, and the result was the 1969 film *Royal Family*.

It was Prince Philip who had always promoted the idea of television as a medium through which the monarchy could pass on its message – in this case, both the 'relentlessness' of the Queen's job, and the fact that she was by no means the one-dimensional figure more traditional coverage was making her appear. The Queen was at first reluctant but allowed herself to be persuaded, and shooting began on 8 June 1968.

Seventy-five days of shooting in 172 locations; 43 hours of film that would be cut down to 110 minutes. The Queen was shown working on her red dispatch boxes at Sandringham, at Balmoral, on *Britannia* and on the Royal Train; abroad on state visits; giving lunch to President Nixon; receiving the Prime Minister for his weekly audience. The film also showed Prince Charles water-skiing and working on his college history essay; Prince Philip piloting a plane and painting a watercolour. And it showed the Queen herself riding, watching a

A relaxed moment at Windsor for the Queen and her eldest son.

The 1969 fly-on-the-wall documentary *Royal Family* saw cameras follow the royals for
several months as they went about their daily business. Inevitably, however, scenes like
this family lunch at Windsor can seem rather stilted.

sitcom on television, driving her children out in a Land Rover and helping with a
family barbecue.

The consciously ordinary atmosphere of the barbecue, the stodginess of clothes and
tastes, must have seemed reassuring. But was it perhaps a little disappointing, too?
Prince Philip believed that if people could see their head of state and her close family
'as individuals, as people, I think it makes it much easier for them to accept the
system.' He was all against the idea of any 'remoteness or majesty' in the people's
view of their monarchy. But many others disagreed. Walter Bagehot, writing of the
monarchy a century earlier, had said 'We must not let in daylight upon magic,' and
even David Attenborough, one of *Royal Family*'s producers, believed they would
suffer from the loss of mystique.

More than two-thirds of the population of Britain watched *Royal Family*
– but the Queen has since ordered that it be withdrawn from view.

Nevertheless, 23 million people watched *Royal Family* when it aired on the BBC
in black and white on 21 June 1969 – another 15 million when ITV showed it in
colour. Even allowing for repeat viewers, more than half of the population of
Britain must have seen the film, and the reception across the Atlantic was
equally enthusiastic.

From the modernity of a broadcast media appearance to what looked, at least, like
a medieval ceremony . . . the Royal Family were eager to show that they could
play both cards. Ten days after the film was shown Prince Charles was invested
as Prince of Wales in the courtyard of Caernarfon Castle. With his youthful face
incongruous above the ermine and velvet cape, he knelt before the unromantically
modern-clad figure of his mother and vowed to be her 'liege man of life and limb'.

The ceremony, designed by Princess Margaret's husband, Lord Snowdon, was in fact
a modern creation, and (as the Queen told Noël Coward later) both mother and son
were stifling giggles at the memory of the dress rehearsal, when an over-large crown
had extinguished Charles 'like a candle-snuffer'. But the event, watched by a huge

On 1 July 1969, the Queen invested her son as Prince of Wales at Caernarfon Castle. Despite the formality of the ceremony, the family joked among themselves that the crown, before it was adjusted to fit, looked like a candle-snuffer on Charles' head.

audience worldwide, did give another feelgood factor – and such were desperately needed in what were revealing themselves as alarmingly changing times.

One element in the reinvention of the royals over the preceding century had been to present them (under Prince Albert's guidance) as the nation's first family, an ideal of middle-class morality. But now that very ideal seemed out of sync with the age of free love and of feminism.

Small wonder, perhaps, that the painter Pietro Annigoni, returning to make another portrait of the Queen in 1969, found her both frailer and harder than when he first painted her fourteen years before. He told the Queen he saw her as condemned to solitude by her position, and that was how he planned to show her. She was content to go along with his vision, whether or not she agreed. 'One doesn't know oneself,' she once said.

The Queen once regretted that, unlike her mother, she had as she aged the kind of face that looked sulky in repose. Watching herself on television, she exclaimed to Philip that she had on 'my Miss Piggy face'! The feelings with which so many refuse to credit her make things, if anything, worse. Said Labour parliamentarian Richard Crossman: 'When she is deeply moved and tries to conceal it, she looks like an angry thunder-cloud.' And there was, by the early 1970s, a certain amount to look angry about.

In 1970, the Conservative but uncongenial Edward Heath replaced Harold Wilson. He too came to value his audiences with the Queen. 'The fact that she has all these years of experience and is imperturbable is a source of encouragement in itself,' Heath said, noting that as someone who had met and corresponded with so many world leaders she was particularly good 'on overseas stuff'.

It was Heath who took Britain into the Common Market, the European Economic Community, and perhaps thus weakened ties with the Commonwealth, so dear to the Queen's heart. In 1974, Wilson was once more returned to power – but by then the Queen had problems closer to home.

In March of that year there was a terrifying attempt to kidnap Princess Anne at gunpoint while she was being driven along the Mall. The Queen is notably cool about personal danger. When, seven years later, six blank shots were fired at her as she rode to the Trooping of the Colour ceremony, her only reaction was to reassure her horse. And when, the year after that, the disturbed Michael Fagan broke into her bedroom, she held the intruder in conversation until the alarm could be raised. But the armed kidnap attempt on one of her children must have shaken her.

Her sister's marriage was in difficulties. Lord Snowdon was a serial womanizer. Princess Margaret, too, had already reputedly sought consolation outside her marriage, and in 1973 she was introduced to Roddy Llewellyn, seventeen years her junior, with whom she would go on to have an open affair that lasted for almost a decade. The relationship between husband and wife had become vicious, to the point where he would leave her notes reading 'Things I Hate About You'. It did not help that the press were no longer prepared, as in bygone decades, to maintain a degree of gentlemanly discretion – not, at least, the new boy on the scene, Rupert Murdoch, owner of the *Sun* and *News of the World*.

These were difficult years all round, not least because of the economic clime – galloping inflation, a falling stock market, oil prices doubling, and the clash between government and trade unions that culminated in the three-day week, with its system of compulsory closures and sporadic blackouts. Other territories in the Commonwealth, of which the Queen was always very much aware, had their own problems; notably the terrible famine in Bangladesh.

The Queen's Christmas message at the end of 1974 sounded an uncharacteristically downbeat note. 'We have never been short of problems, but in the last year everything seems to have happened at once . . . The trouble with gloom is that it feeds upon itself and depression causes more depression . . . In times of doubt and anxiety, the attitudes people show in their daily lives, in their homes, and in their work, are of supreme importance.'

This, of course, had always been her theme. Business as usual, and not just as a matter of practicality, but as a duty. Look for the rays of sunshine where you can.

And as Princess Anne reached maturity, the Queen must have taken pleasure in the fact that at least one of her older children was finding her feet – and in a way that was particularly congenial to Her Majesty.

By the time of her Christmas broadcast in 1971, the Queen had become well-accustomed to the microphone.

Horses and Dogs

The Queen cantering up to the start of the track at Royal Ascot race course, where she used to enjoy a private ride with her family.

As the 1970s dawned, Princess Anne was using the freedom now accorded to a royal to pursue an equestrian career. Emancipated from school at Benenden, entering her twenties, she celebrated the new decade by winning the individual title at the European Eventing Championship, and being voted BBC Sports Personality of the Year in 1971.

In 1976, Anne would compete as one of the British team at the Olympic Games in Montreal, riding the Queen's horse Goodwill. It is, of course, a passion – and a proficiency at international level – that Anne's own daughter, Zara, has come to share, just as the Queen's interest was inherited from her father.

Horses have always been the passion of the Queen's life. It started early – her cousin Margaret Rhodes recalled that as children they played endlessly at being horses, at Elizabeth's desire, 'and it was obligatory to neigh'. It's a passion which has kept her in the saddle into old age, still refusing to wear the almost mandatory hard hat, and it seems telling that it is the world of the stable which permits the only known display of rebellion on the part of this most dutiful lady.

Her horses, like her dogs, allow her an element of being ordinary. They have, after all, no sense of monarchy or ceremony. They respond not to her rank, but to her abilities.

The family that plays together, stays together . . . The Royal Family
posing for the camera before riding at Windsor in 1957.

Horses, she herself said once, 'are the greatest levellers in the world'.

Riding, of course, has been a traditional pastime for the upper classes; and the young
Elizabeth and Margaret were far from the only children of privilege to tack and
groom their ponies themselves. But Princess Elizabeth was unusual in having been
able to share with her father visits to his racing stables, talking to the trainers and
jockeys and learning the skilful matching of qualities and track records that might
breed a winner.

As a child she was lucky, though not unusual, in having two riding lessons a week.
What was, again, unusual was that, from the time of her father's accession to the
throne, she was given lessons in riding sidesaddle, as well as astride. The arcane skill
would be necessary when, as sovereign, she had to balance on a sidesaddle holding
crop and reins in one hand, the other raised in a salute, as she surveyed the annual
ceremony of Trooping the Colour.

It is only since 1987 that she has watched the ceremony from a horse-drawn carriage,
and that was more to do with the retirement of her black mare Burmese than with
any acknowledgement of anno domini. In her eighties, the Queen still continued to
ride for pleasure whenever her schedule allowed, albeit on a sure-footed Fell pony
rather than the larger mounts she used to prefer.

Windsor is the base from which she can watch proceedings at the Royal Windsor Horse Show – she won a prize, for the single private driving class, at the second show in 1944 – and at the Guards Polo Club. Her appearance at Royal Ascot is a behatted public fixture, but out of the public eye she and other members of the Royal Family used also to enjoy a private race with each other along five furlongs of Ascot track. Her mother (whose racing expenses she often paid) shared her preoccupation with racing, albeit that the Queen Mother as an owner leaned more towards National Hunt racing, while the Queen breeds for the flat.

Those who work in the Queen's racing stables (around Sandringham and Hampton Court, and in Berkshire) say her interest in breeding and training is that of a professional. She is said to read the Racing Post over breakfast every morning and has an encyclopedic knowledge of the stud book. Making her own photographic record of mares and their foals at Sandringham, she is prepared even for the challenging world of the covering shed and is happy to stand out for chilly early hours on the gallops. She has usually about twenty-five horses in training each season, racing in the royal silks: royal purple with scarlet sleeves and a black velvet cap. Her pleasure in watching them is visible to everyone and she is not above having a bet. 'One has perhaps the gambling instinct,' as she says.

The Queen had a stream of winners in the first years of her reign. She was Britain's top money winner in 1954 and 1957, thanks in part to Aureole, the horse for which she had been so concerned on Coronation Day. In the event, the temperamental Aureole was beaten into second place that year but next year won the aptly named Coronation Cup, and the King George VI and Queen Elizabeth Stakes, going on to become a two-time champion sire.

The 1960s were less successful racing years for the Queen, but 1974 (soon after Princess Anne married fellow equestrian

The Queen has always enjoyed a strong rapport with horses, relishing the fact that the animals have no idea of her royal status.

Mark Phillips in a big public ceremony), brought the repeated successes of her filly Highclere. When, on a visit to America, she was given her first computer, the use she found for it was to keep track of all the information on her bloodstock. Although racing is a business, the Queen takes a more personal approach.

With an instinctive understanding of horses, she displayed great interest in the training techniques of 'horse whisperer' Monty Roberts, once snatching a whole week from her schedule to watch him at work and making the California cowboy a genuine friend. Time out to spend with horses and horse people, in bluegrass country or in the West, has always featured heavily

The Queen can usually be found surrounded by corgis and 'dorgis' (a corgi/dachshund cross) – as here, arriving at Aberdeen Airport to start her holiday at Balmoral in 1974.

in her enjoyment of the USA. A courtier who saw the Queen on one of her visits to her Kentucky friends, Will and Sarah Farish, spoke of how much she relished 'an atmosphere of informality and gaiety that I never saw in England'.

The Queen is almost as famous for her love of dogs as of horses, and though she exercises a notably firm control over the gun dogs on her various estates, the corgis inside her palaces are treated with more indulgence. Visitors are sometimes taken aback when the Queen enters a room surrounded by, as Princess Diana once put it, a 'moving carpet' of fur. Her corgi Susan went on honeymoon with her, and all her corgis since have been Susan's descendants. Since one of her corgis bred with Princess Margaret's dachshund Pipkin, she has also had a number of dorgis, a corgi/dachshund cross. When the Queen Mother died, the Queen took on her corgis – but in recent years she herself has refrained from breeding any new young dogs.

Prince Philip's feelings for horses are less visceral. Polo was a sport he took up after his marriage, and relished for its pace and fierce competitive edge. When in the 1970s arthritis made polo impossible, he took to carriage driving with equal verve. He and his wife, after all, were now in their middle years. The Queen had already reigned longer than most of her predecessors, for all that, as we now know, this would prove to be only the first act in the long story of her reign.

Home and Away

The 1970s were difficult times, both for the country and the monarchy. It was in full awareness of that difficulty that Palace and politicians began discussion of how best to celebrate the Silver Jubilee which, in 1977, saw the Queen mark twenty-five years on the throne.

Prime Minister James Callaghan was dubious as to how much attention should be paid in view of the appalling economic climate, the Queen herself was anxious no one should be forced into spending money. But (just as when her wedding had been discussed, thirty years before) an alternative school of thought held that this would be a welcome spot of colour – and that the cheer should be spread not only through the country, but the Commonwealth.

The Queen and Prince Philip were aboard the royal yacht *Britannia* when, in 1977, they were entertained by Fijian folk musicians and dancers.

In the second week of February, the
Queen and Prince Philip set off aboard
the Royal Yacht *Britannia* to the Pacific
Islands, New Zealand and Australia.
It was the first of two great tours that
year; the second, in the autumn took her
to the Caribbean and to Canada. The
royal couple would travel some 56,000
miles that year, greeted everywhere by
crowds the size and enthusiasm of
which defied gloomy predictions.

In New Zealand, she was photographed
beaming broadly and dressed in a Maori
fur cloak. In the Bahamas, she was seen
sampling fruit off a market stall. In Fiji,
she was spotted snatching the chance to
repair her lipstick while crowds were
distracted when a roof collapsed during
a demonstration of native dance.

One of the more unusual welcomes to the Queen
received came in Tuvalu, in 1982, when she was carried
ashore in a canoe by islanders.

She has over the years been photographed
aboard a stunningly caparisoned elephant; borne high on the shoulders of Tuvalu
islanders in a native canoe; addressing a gathering of more than a quarter of a million
in India; on the Great Wall of China; in floor-length black lace with a mantilla and
pearls for a meeting with Pope John XXIII; in socks exiting the Golden Temple of
Amritsar. The meticulous planning of a tour is printed in a pocket-sized booklet called
The Blue Book (or, jokingly, 'The Bible') carried by each member of her entourage.

The Queen's visits to the Americas alone have provided some notable memories.
It has been for her a land of opportunity. During her first visit as Queen in 1957,
she had made her first live television broadcast ('shy, a bit bashful, and sometimes
awkward' – but all the more endearing for it, said the *New York Times*), her first game
of American football – and her first visit to a supermarket, an invention which had
not yet reached Britain. (The royal pair were amazed at the choice of goods available,

as they peered into shopping trolleys and chatted with customers.) The Queen had asked to approach New York from the water, and as she saw the Manhattan skyline, she said 'Wheeeee!' Touring the UN headquarters, she asked how the glass skyscrapers 'kept standing up'.

The Queen has always been drawn to the freedom and adventure of North America. She was fascinated when, on the royal tour of 1957, she was taken to the 86th floor of the Empire State Building.

On that trip, a much-desired visit to the West Coast had been cut from her schedule. A quarter of a century later, a Californian president, Ronald Reagan, would give her the opportunity. Unseasonal rain meant the royal couple had to be transported in a Navy bus – another first – but she got to dine on the soundstage at 20th Century Fox and to fly low over the Golden Gate Bridge.

More seriously, ever since her visit to South Africa as a young woman, ever since that first Commonwealth tour, foreign trips have continued to be a vital part of her queenship. Elizabeth II's foreign tours have made her the most travelled monarch in history, something the rise of air travel has made a possibility.

(Opposite) Greeting King Khalid on a visit to Saudi Arabia in 1979, the Queen's long dress is a gesture to the customs of the country. (Right) Taking an elephant ride while touring India in 1961.

Not all tours are foreign ones: the Queen is pictured during a London walkabout on the occasion of her 1977 Silver Jubilee.

They are a way to bind together the Commonwealth countries, a way to repair diplomatic damage, or to celebrate an alliance. Like the official visits she hosts for foreign visitors, the Queen's foreign tours represent an important stake in Britain's bid for a continuing place at the top table of international diplomacy. Her realm may loom less large than it used to on the international stage, but perhaps no other visitor in the world can give so much cachet.

The schedules can be punishing. When Jackie Kennedy once complained to her of how tiring she had found a tour, the Queen remarked that, 'One gets crafty after a while and learns how to save oneself.' She travelled by Concorde on the last leg of the 1977 Commonwealth tours – a gesture to the future and to innovation, but also a speedy way home.

Not all tours, however, are foreign ones, by any means. In her 1977 Jubilee year, the Queen was determined to see as much of Britain as possible, and that Britain would see her. 'I have to be seen to be believed,' she said once. The Queen and Prince Philip toured thirty-six UK counties over three months and (in defiance of the early fears the Jubilee celebrations might meet with a lacklustre response) a million people came out on one day in Lancashire alone. Trestle tables were being set up, food being baked, for more than twelve thousand street parties across Britain.

On 4 May, the Queen travelled to Parliament for 'Loyal Addresses' from both Houses. There, in response to recent calls for more devolved powers to the other nations of her realm, she made an unusually direct political comment. 'I cannot forget that I was

crowned Queen of the United Kingdom of Great Britain and Northern Ireland. Perhaps this Jubilee is a time to remind ourselves of the benefits which union has conferred . . .' Perhaps it was in that spirit that the last stop on her UK tour was Northern Ireland, a territory she hadn't visited in eleven years, and a visit that was considered deeply risky in the context of the Troubles.

The Queen and other members of the Royal Family celebrated 25 years of her reign with a service at St Paul's Cathedral.

The centrepiece of the Jubilee celebrations was more conventional. On 7 June, a million people gathered in London to watch the carriage procession from Buckingham Palace to St Paul's. The Queen and Prince Philip rode in the Gold State Coach: 24 feet long, weighing 4 tons, and taking eight horses to pull it at a walk. Other members of the Royal Family rode in the Irish State Coach, Queen Alexandra's State Coach and the Glass Coach – but, after all that pomp, came a royal walkabout, with stops to chat. Elizabeth had been genuinely touched and surprised by the welcome of the crowds. Though the punk rock group the Sex Pistols sailed down the Thames playing their 'God Save the Queen', in mocking counterpoise to the official barge procession, theirs was almost a lone voice of dissent.

'When I was twenty-one I pledged my life to the service of our people,' the Queen said in a Jubilee speech, 'and I asked God's help to make good that vow. Although that vow was made in my salad days, when I was green in judgement, I do not regret nor retract one word of it.' The Archbishop of Canterbury, in St Paul's, had praised her as an example 'of service untiringly done, of duty faithfully fulfilled'.

This much was true – but the Archbishop also spoke 'of a home life stable and wonderfully happy'. This would prove to be the difficulty in the years ahead. Though November of Jubilee year brought the birth of the Queen's first grandchild, Peter Phillips, in the following year her sister Margaret's divorce was finalized. As the monarchy entered the last quarter of the twentieth century, there were too many question marks over the years ahead.

The End of the Fairy Tale

On 4 May 1979, Margaret Thatcher became Prime Minister, following Labour's James Callaghan. That summer the Royal Family suffered a devastating blow. On 27 August the IRA blew up the sailing boat belonging to Lord Louis Mountbatten, killing Mountbatten himself, several members of his family and a local boy, and seriously injuring others. The seventy-nine-year-old Mountbatten – Prince Phillip's uncle and a former Viceroy of India – was a divisive figure whose closest royal relationship was probably with Prince Charles, who regarded him as a mentor. The impact on the heir to the throne was devastating . . . But Ireland was not the only difficult issue of the Thatcher years.

Of all the dealings with Prime Ministers the Queen has had during her reign, this is the relationship that has attracted most attention. It is often said that the royal lady and the 'Iron Lady' did not get on, but that is probably stating it too personally. The Queen has on several occasions spoken in support of women's abilities, of other women's entitlement to positions of authority. It is perhaps true that the Queen's own concerns were out of sync with the hard-nosed feel of the Thatcher era.

The two had a point of difference in the Commonwealth (which Mrs Thatcher, like Heath before her, was disinclined to take seriously) and its policy of sanctions against South Africa. A report in the *Sunday Times*, sourced from the Palace press secretary, even painted the Queen as an 'astute political infighter' quite prepared to tackle Downing Street over its uncaring attitudes to race and social diversity.

But Mrs Thatcher was wholly a monarchist – even if she did usurp some of the prerogatives of monarchy. With the Falklands War in 1982, it was Mrs Thatcher who took the official role in welcoming home the victorious troops . . . for all that the Royal Family have always had a particularly strong connection with the military. Indeed, during the Falklands War the Queen's second son, Prince Andrew, saw active service with the Royal Navy, something the Queen is likely to have taken with the fortitude of a long-established Service family.

The Queen's eldest son was also in the news – but for matters of love, not war. In 1980, the thirty-one-year-old Prince Charles encountered the nineteen-year-old Lady Diana Spencer, youngest daughter of Earl Spencer, at a weekend house party. Charles was still feeling the effects of Mountbatten's death; and it had been Mountbatten who had urged him to marry – and urged that, while a young man should sow his wild oats, for his bride Charles should 'choose a suitable, attractive and sweet-charactered girl before she met anyone else she might fall for'.

The pair had met in earlier years when Charles had been involved with Diana's elder sister Sarah, but then Diana had been a mere sixteen. Now Diana – unhappy at home, thanks to her parents' bitter divorce and her father's remarriage to romantic novelist Barbara Cartland's daughter Raine – was looking for her path in life. Without a qualification to her name ('thick', she cheerfully called herself), she saw marriage as the obvious option.

That autumn the press spotted Diana sitting beside Charles as he fished the river Dee and immediately took up the tale of 'Shy Di'; the aristocratic English rose, working as a kindergarten assistant in her frilly blouses and her Laura Ashley skirts. Her uncle Lord Fermoy assured the press she was a virgin; her biographer Andrew Morton would describe her telling him she knew she had to 'keep myself tidy'.

Prince Charles and Lady Diana Spencer announced their engagement on 24 February 1981, Charles telling a friend he wanted to do 'the right thing for this Country'. Yes, of course the pair were in love 'whatever "in love" means . . .' he told reporters. With hindsight, there were too many indications that this would end badly. But at the time – 'It was a fairy story and everyone wanted it to work,' said Diana later, ruefully.

The couple were married on 29 July 1981 – and in St Paul's, since Westminster Abbey could not hold the long list of foreign notables invited to the huge public ceremony. The Queen was only one of those who felt that at a time of unemployment, IRA violence and rioting, it would cheer the country – just as her own wedding had done, in the aftermath of war. And if the enormous meringue of a wedding dress the Emmanuels designed for Diana was distinctly crumpled as she emerged from the car on to the steps of St Paul's – if she did slightly fumble Charles's names at the altar – those were the only things wrong with the day.

Patrick Lichfield captured this behind-the-scenes image of the wedding of
Prince Charles and Lady Diana Spencer. The Queen looks on as Diana speaks
to her young bridesmaids.

But Prince Charles later told Jonathan Dimbleby it was on honeymoon on board
Britannia that he first learned Diana suffered from the eating disorder bulimia.
This was, however, not shared with press and public, who saw a very different story.

At the beginning of November, the Palace announced that the Princess of Wales was
pregnant. Prince William was born on 21 June 1982, after less than a year of his
parents' marriage. Diana said later that she had 'felt the whole country was in labour
with me'. The couple's second son, Prince Harry, followed on 15 September 1984.

Diana's approach to child-rearing would come to dramatize her differences from the
Royal Family. Everyone remembers the 1980s photographs of Diana, flying to hug her
sons after a separation – and contrasts them with the 1950s image of a young Prince
Charles, exchanging a solemn handshake with his mother as the Queen returned
from her first Commonwealth tour.

Charles and Diana appear on the balcony of Buckingham Palace. At the time, it seemed as though this was a fairy-tale romance.

Diana's transformation from shy Sloane into glamorous icon had begun, moreover. Blonde, blue-eyed and ever more stylish, she evoked the romantic image of the fairy-tale princess. By the US visit of 1985 – where Diana danced with John Travolta – she was, Reader's Digest declared afterwards, 'The World's Number One Celebrity'.

Both partners in the marriage, however, were unhappy. And both had now begun to look for support elsewhere. It was probably in 1986 that Charles's longstanding romance with Camilla Parker Bowles resumed its sexual aspect (causing Diana later to complain, famously, that there were three people in her marriage).

In the same year Diana's personal bodyguard, Barry Mannakee, was transferred to other duties, amid hints that he had grown too close, and she met Life Guardsman James Hewitt. Also in 1986 the marriage of the Queen's second son, Prince Andrew, the Duke of York, to Sarah Ferguson provided a welcome distraction for the press, and gave Diana the support of another outsider within the Royal Family.

But it was to no avail. At the end of her eighteen-month affair with Hewitt – when Diana moved on to James Gilbey – the troubled marriage of the Waleses had effectively foundered.

Palaces and Parties

Ask any child what a queen does, and they'll say she wears a crown, and lives in a palace . . . Or, in the case of Queen Elizabeth II, a number of palaces, actually. Buckingham Palace is the name most of us first associate with royalty – with its nineteen state rooms, fifty-two principal bedrooms, plus 188 for the staff, post office, cinema, doctor's surgery and 40 acres of enclosed garden carved out of the centre of London, an oasis of lakes and lawns.

The creation of Buckingham Palace from a far more modest house was begun under George IV, but Queen Victoria was the first monarch to live there. It has been the Royal Family's official London residence since 1837, and the refusal of George VI and his wife to move out during the wartime Blitz was an important boost to morale. But when her father's accession to the throne forced the family to move there from 145 Piccadilly, the young Princess Elizabeth and her sister were dismayed – and there is still a sense that the Palace is more the monarchy's office than its true home.

If Buckingham Palace is the head of the monarchy, Windsor Castle is its heart. The original castle was built soon after the Norman Conquest, making it the longest-occupied palace in Europe. It bears the marks of all those years. In the fifteenth-century St George's Chapel, the Queen's parents and grandparents are buried – along with her sister, Princess Margaret – beside earlier monarchs including Edward IV and Henry VIII.

Windsor was remodelled after the Restoration of 1660 and again in the Georgian eras, and extensively rebuilt after the devastating fire of 1992 ripped through a hundred rooms. The distress felt then by the Queen shows the importance of a place which enshrines so much of her family's history. Besides the castle itself, much of Windsor – the whole 655-acre Home Park – is essentially a family enclave, with smaller houses that can be apportioned at the Queen's pleasure, the royal mausoleum at Frogmore, and the private golf course where Prince Andrew plays.

From her favourite position astride a horse, the Queen
points towards Balmoral – her favourite home.

The Palace of Holyroodhouse in Edinburgh is the official residence of the British
monarch in Scotland, but the Queen usually spends only one week a year there, to
carry out official duties. Far more time is pleasurably spent at Balmoral Castle, which
(unlike Holyroodhouse, Buckingham Palace or Windsor) is not part of the nationally
owned Crown Estate but a piece of private property.

Balmoral was purchased in 1852 by Queen Victoria who built the house as a Scots
Baronial fantasy. Victoria's love of the Highlands is shared by the present family, who
often wear tartan while there, and dance reels with their gamekeepers at the twice-
yearly Ghillies' Ball. The Queen has always chosen to spend August, September
and part of October here. No coincidence that this is the shooting season – life at
Balmoral, and the 50,000 acre working estate which surrounds it, revolves around the
pursuit of deer, grouse and salmon. Prince Philip has always been a keen fisherman,
who himself taught his children to shoot, besides enjoying sailing in Scottish waters.

More surprisingly, the Queen, too, has since childhood been an expert stalker. It is
now more than thirty years since she last shot a stag, but the messy business of

gralloching the animal – gutting it, so the Balmoral ponies can more easily carry it home to the larder – holds no terrors for her. The Queen loves the interior of Balmoral, saying it is 'rather fun' to keep it as Queen Victoria left it, with thistle-patterned wallpaper, tartan rugs, and rows of antlers on the wall. But perhaps even more she loves riding and walking among the purple heather, the burns, and the firs.

Like Balmoral, Sandringham House in Norfolk has been a private property of the Royal Family since the middle of the nineteenth century, when Queen Victoria bought it for her son the Prince of Wales. A neo-Jacobean mansion of red brick, it too boasts excellent shooting and riding opportunities. (Edward VII and George V kept the clocks at Sandringham half an hour ahead of Greenwich Mean Time, to allow more daylight hours for sport.) The estate also boasts 16,000 acres of farmland, producing apples and other crops for sale, besides being home to the Royal Stud, and the loft for the Queen's racing pigeons.

One beloved 'home' – for that is how they saw it – has been gained and lost by the Royal Family within the Queen's reign. The Royal Yacht *Britannia*, commissioned by her father and launched in 1953, was decommissioned in 1997 and is now moored in

The Queen's life often requires formal dress, but boots, tartan skirt, waterproofs and headscarf are her preferred 'uniform' for holidays at Balmoral.

Edinburgh's port of Leith as a tourist attraction. But over more than forty years *Britannia* took the Queen on almost seven hundred trips abroad, notching up more than a million nautical miles. At once a 'country house at sea' and a floating palace, the ship could accommodate foreign receptions in a helpfully cosy and British atmosphere, besides providing a honeymoon retreat for the Queen's sister and three of her children.

In an age of helicopters, and of a cost-cutting monarchy, the future of the Royal Train (a set of specially fitted carriages which can be pulled by either of two locomotives) must also be in doubt. But perhaps in any case its

The royal yacht *Britannia*, decommissioned in 1997, was a much-loved retreat for the Royal Family, and particularly for the Queen. It also served as something of a floating embassy, carrying the Queen on tours and acting as a base in which she could receive foreign dignitaries.

comparatively spartan 1970s fittings would not appeal to a younger generation. It comes as a surprise that in their private rooms, the taste of the elder royals in many ways reflects the unfashionable decor of their youth, which often looks dowdy today. But they can certainly turn on the grandeur when need be. Magnificence is, of course, an important weapon in their nation's diplomatic armoury.

The Queen has hosted more than a hundred State Banquets in the course of her reign. Preparation is meticulous, beginning as much as six months ahead, and the Queen herself checks all details of what is in every sense a polished production. For a banquet at Windsor, the table is so wide that footmen have to walk down the middle with dusters on their feet to place flowers and candelabra.

Dress is white tie – or national dress, which can provide some colourful alternatives, as when the President of Ghana visited Buckingham Palace in 2007. In May 2011, President and Michelle Obama were served sole in crayfish sauce, Windsor lamb, sauteed courgettes and radishes, green beans, potatoes and salad, followed by a vanilla and cherry charlotte. Before the meal the Queen proposes a toast to her visitor, who reciprocates. A military orchestra dispenses music until the swirl of pipers signals the end of the meal.

A State Banquet is the centrepiece of a full State Visit, lasting three or five days and beginning with a ceremonial welcome complete with military guard of honour and marching bands. Not all official visits are state visits – of all the US Presidents who have held office during the Queen's reign, only two, George W. Bush and Barack Obama, have made full State Visits. But other American visitors have enjoyed other pleasures.

In 1982, for example, Ronald and Nancy Reagan, staying at Windsor as personal guests, found their seven-room suite had been equipped with a dedicated White House

The dress code for state dinners requires white tie – or national dress – as worn by Ghanaian President John Agyekum Kufuor in 2007, when the Queen formally welcomed him to a banquet marking the 50th anniversary of Ghanaian independence.

On 15 June 1961, the Queen and Prince Philip hosted a banquet in honour of US President John F. Kennedy and his wife Jackie.

The Queen and the cowboy – Elizabeth and US President Ronald Reagan riding out
together in the grounds of Windsor Castle in 1982. The Queen's horse Burmese
(who carried her many times at Trooping the Colour) was, like the President's mount
Centennial, a gift from the Canadian Mounted Police.

telephone line and Windsor Castle's first ever shower. The centrepiece of this visit
was the ride the Queen and President took together in Windsor Great Park, while
Prince Philip drove Nancy Reagan in a four-in-hand carriage.

Visitors who come to Windsor for a 'dine and sleep' find a footman or housemaid assigned to help them prepare for drinks in one of the huge drawing rooms. Then comes a change into formal dress before assembling at 8.15 for dinner in the State Dining Room. Their royal hosts join the party a quarter of an hour later, and at dinner the Queen maintains the old protocol of talking to her partner on one side through the first course, and then changing to the other. In the castle library, carefully selected objects of interest are laid out to admire, before the Queen herself leads a tour through the castle's staggering art collection. After goodbyes are said at night the guests do not see their hosts again.

But in a private setting, the Queen could in her younger days be something of a party animal, declaring – as at 1.30 a.m. she left the wedding 'breakfast' she hosted after Charles and Diana's wedding – that she'd have loved to stay and dance all night. A month earlier, throwing Prince Andrew a twenty-first birthday disco party at Windsor, she gave Elton John 'one of the most surreal moments of my life' when she joined the younger guests dancing in a circle to 'Rock Around the Clock'.

Christmases at Sandringham are a riot of joke presents, charades (the Queen is a good mimic) and party games of the old-fashioned physical sort. At Balmoral, visitors find the Queen acting as an attentive hostess, herself checking their bedrooms. After the day's sport it is she who makes tea, with water from a silver urn; playing a game of patience as the company assemble for drinks before dinner.

Tony Blair was struck by the strength of the drinks – 'true rocket fuel', he said. But then successive Prime Ministers have been taken aback by life at Balmoral. John Major once found his phone call to a European leader during a political crisis drowned out by the sound of the bagpipes which play at regular intervals. Mrs Thatcher, after one of the picnics which famously see Prince Philip at the barbecue and the Queen washing up, sent a present of a pair of rubber gloves. It seems a world away from a State Banquet – but perhaps that very combination is the secret of the Queen's hospitality.

Part III
Change and Celebration
1986–2016

(Clockwise from top right) The Queen after the blessing of her son Charles' marriage to Camilla Parker Bowles; walking behind the coffin at the funeral of her mother; and pictured on the balcony of Buckingham Palace with her son, grandson and great-grandson.

Anni Horribiles

In 1987 the Queen honoured her daughter with the title of Princess Royal, which since the seventeenth century could be bestowed on (and only on) the eldest daughter of a sovereign. Anne's stalwart dignity and formidable record of public works had done much to change earlier perceptions of her as brusque and unsympathetic.

However, a decade on from the Silver Jubilee, time was about to prove less kind to the Royal Family as a whole. Courtiers soon begun to talk about QVS or the Queen Victoria Syndrome, whereby a nation could become tired of an ageing monarch and an extensive and expensive Royal Family.

The administration and financing of Buckingham Palace were under review; and adverse publicity came when Prince Edward's decision in January 1987 to drop out of the Marines training course was followed by his first venture into television. The Queen (reluctant to disappoint her son) gave dubious consent to what was meant to be a light-hearted romp in aid of charity. But *It's a Royal Knockout* made those younger members of the family who gamely took part in it look like pantomime figures.

The Queen herself was not immune from the general disatissfaction. Her predecessor Queen Victoria had done far more to deserve the hostility that came her way. After Prince Albert's death in 1861, she withdrew into seclusion. Her refusal to meet her ministers alone, to attend every event of importance, from the Privy Council meeting and the State Opening of Parliament to her own son's wedding party gave – in the words of her minister Lord Halifax – 'some evidence of insanity'.

By contrast, Elizabeth II has always been distinguished by her sense of duty. Nonetheless, a poll at the beginning of 1990 had nearly half the population supporting the idea of an 'eventual' abdication.

But the next generation, too, were experiencing difficulties. By the end of the 1980s, all the marriages of the Queen's children were in trouble to a greater or lesser degree. In the spring of 1989, the *Sun* published love letters exchanged some time earlier between Princess Anne and Commander Timothy Laurence. That year, she and her husband Mark Phillips announced their separation.

The Duke and Duchess of York produced two daughters, the Princesses Beatrice and Eugenie, in 1988 and 1990 respectively. But the Duchess was beginning to chafe at the restrictions of life of a secondary royal. At the end of 1991, Andrew and 'Fergie' told the Queen they were considering a separation.

And beyond all the rest, by now, of course, everyone was aware of the 'War of the Waleses' – the very public breakdown of the heir to the throne's marriage. The time for discretion was past. Back in the autumn of 1987, the Queen had summoned the pair to Buckingham Palace and privately urged them, effectively, to do what her generation would have done – to put a brave face on things, and sort themselves out behind the scenes. And, up to a point, they had tried.

Charles based himself at Highgrove and Diana at Kensington Palace, while they concentrated on their respective charitable endeavours. But it cannot have helped that Diana – visiting hospices and orphanages, embracing lepers and AIDS victims – was getting literally ten times the press coverage that was given to Charles's work. She was winning the public relations war.

Before the time came to trumpet the tenth anniversary of the royal couple's wedding, the game was up. Diana was already secretly collaborating with the biographer Andrew Morton.

That was even before 1992 got underway – what the Queen called her annus horribilis. And arguably the fact that she did so in Latin displayed all too clearly the problem of the Royal Family.

January brought revelations about Fergie and the millionaire Steve Wyatt. In February, what was meant to be a journey of reconciliation for the Waleses saw Diana photographed ostentatiously alone, in what the *Daily Mail* called 'wistful solitude', in front of the Taj Mahal. In March it was announced the Yorks would separate; in April,

The photograph of Diana, ostentatiously alone in front of the Taj Mahal, came to symbolize the disarray which, by the early 1990s, had overtaken the marital affairs of the next generation of the Royal Family.

Princess Anne's divorce from Captain Mark Phillips became final; in June Prince Edward was forced to deny rumours of homosexuality.

Also in June came Andrew Morton's *Diana: Her True Story*, written (though she denied it at the time) with the cooperation of the Princess. Its indictment of Charles as an unfeeling husband seemed to represent a problem at the heart of the monarchy. Diana's butler, Paul Burrell, later described how the possibility of a split was mooted, but the Queen and Prince Philip, holding a crisis meeting with the younger couple at Windsor, urged greater efforts. That they should be 'less selfish' – should think of the monarchy, their children, their country.

August brought photographs of the Duchess of York having her toes sucked by her 'financial adviser' John Bryan. It also, and more seriously, saw the publication of the 'Squidgygate' tapes – conversations three years before between Diana ('Squidgy') and James Gilbey, in which Diana made clear her hostility to the Royal Family. The Queen, as she admitted to friends, was proving unlucky in her daughters-in-law. The War of the Waleses represented the clash of two cultures, with the old ideals of duty, of marriage for life – of a degree of pragmatism in personal affairs – at odds with a newer world. Perhaps that is why the Queen (widely seen as representing the former) was caught in the middle, and why public sympathy for Diana translated into a wider dissatisfaction with the monarchy. Discussions had begun several months earlier about the Queen's paying taxes. But events were to overtake her advisers.

Not the least telling event of 1992 came on 20 November, the Queen and Prince Philip's forty-fifth wedding anniversary, when fire seriously damaged Windsor Castle. When the Queen arrived to see the devastation, those close had never seen her more shaken. After the Queen turned to her mother for consolation, she wrote that the visit had made all the difference to her 'sanity'. But the hurt was redoubled when a sullen nation, in the grip of a recession, rejected Prime Minister John Major's instinctive declaration that the nation would be happy to pay for the repairs.

Joined to press calls for the Queen to pay repair bills on what was seen (not altogether accurately) as her own home, were demands that she should pay taxes. Within days came news that she and Prince Charles would pay tax on their incomes from the Duchies of Lancaster and Cornwall respectively; that she would take over responsibility for most of those family members who had formerly been getting a state subsidy; and that the state rooms

The Queen surveying the devastation caused by the fire which ripped through her beloved Windsor Castle in November 1992.

In a speech at the Guildhall a few days later, the Queen famously described 1992 as an 'Annus Horribilis'.

of Buckingham Palace would open to the public to cover the Windsor repair costs.

It was only four days after the Windsor fire that the Queen appeared (hiding a heavy cold) at a Guildhall lunch to mark her forty years on the throne. She told her fellow guests that 1992 was 'not a year on which I shall look back with undiluted pleasure. In the words of one of my more sympathetic correspondents, it has turned out to be an annus horribilis.'

She came close to rebuking her critics when she said that though 'no institution' could or should expect to be free from oversight, 'scrutiny . . . can be just as effective if it is made with a touch of gentleness, good humour and understanding. This sort of questioning can also act, and it should do so, as an effective agent for change.' The last word – change – was one which would occur time and time again in her speeches ahead.

In December, Buckingham Palace announced that, 'with regret, the Prince and Princess of Wales have decided to separate.' The announcement declared that 'their constitutional positions are unaffected,' but it was very difficult to see how a future with Charles and Diana as king and queen could be achieved.

The Queen took her corgis for a walk at Sandringham rather than watch the broadcast in which John Major relayed the news to Parliament. When she returned to the house a member of staff commiserated with her. 'I think you'll find it's all for the best,' the Queen said. It was an example of her stoicism, but also of a refusal to confront emotional problems. It was an attitude born of her age and class, and certainly inherited from her mother, whom members of her household called the 'imperial ostrich'. But the brave face she had been raised to show in public would itself become a difficulty in the years ahead.

Only days later, on a happier note, Princess Anne married Commander Timothy Laurence at Crathie Church near Balmoral (the Church of Scotland, unlike the Church of England, recognizing remarriage after divorce). The ceremony was a notably restrained and private one, the Queen being one of only thirty guests. Her Christmas message declared that though, 'like many other families, we have lived through some difficult days this year,' she would meet the challenges of the new year with 'fresh hope'.

However, any confidence that 1992 would prove to be a unique 'annus horribilis' was misplaced. The plural of 'annus' is 'anni', anni horribiles, and that is what the mid-1990s proved to be.

Only two weeks into 1993 came 'Camillagate', the published transcript of a deeply embarrassing telephone conversation between Charles and his mistress Camilla Parker Bowles. But, despite a riding accident the Queen suffered as 1993 turned to 1994, business went on. A three-week tour of the Caribbean, commemoration of the fiftieth anniversary of the D-Day landings, and time with the US president Bill Clinton, who later wrote of her as someone 'who might under other circumstances have become a successful politician or diplomat. As it was, she had to be both, without quite seeming to be either.'

The Queen Mother's health was becoming a concern. Now in her nineties, she suffered from failing eyesight, lameness and lesions on her legs, but was resistant to any attempt to make her acknowledge her ailments. A lovely letter from the Queen, sent with a special walking stick, bears witness to the family's concern and belies her unemotional public persona: 'Darling Mummy, Your daughters and your nieces would very much like you to TRY this walking stick! It has a magic handle which fits one's hand like a glove and therefore gives one confidence in movement, especially when feeling dizzy!'

Despite the difficulties the Royal Family were facing, crowds gathered to watch
the Red Arrows fly past Buckingham Palace on the 50th anniversary of VE Day.

Trouble of a more invidious sort came from the very heart of the family. On 29 June
1994, Prince Charles appeared in a lengthy televised interview with Jonathan
Dimbleby, in which he admitted infidelity, though insisting it had not taken place
until his marriage had 'irretrievably broken down'. Almost equally wounding, in a
quieter way, was the portrayal that emerged from Dimbleby's subsequent book of the
Queen as a distant, and Prince Philip as a harsh, parent.

The Queen's own hard work continued. In 1992, three years after the fall of the Berlin
Wall, she had been photographed going through the Brandenburg Gate. Now came a
historic visit to the Soviet Union, the first by a British monarch since the 1917
Revolution, then an equally triumphant return after almost fifty years to a South
Africa now free of apartheid.

But an ever more gravely wounded monarchy was now being described by the
Economist as 'an idea whose time has passed'. It seems telling that in May 1995, the
fiftieth anniversary of VE Day, the Queen gave way to doubt as to whether people
would really come to the balcony appearance she, her mother and sister – three of

'we four' who had stood there fifty years ago – were to make. In the event, of course, the wide expanse in front of Buckingham Palace was packed – and the Queen, as a member of her staff noted, was close to tears as she stepped back inside, downing a gin to help her mask her emotion.

And then Diana struck back. The Panorama interview with Martin Bashir aired on 20 November 1995 is still shocking today. During the hour-long interview she confessed to adultery with James Hewitt, described her bulimia and self-harming, and made the famous declaration that there had been 'three people' in her marriage – a clear reference to Camilla Parker Bowles.

She claimed that she hoped only to be queen of people's hearts, but also asserted that Prince Charles was by temperament unsuited to 'the top job'. Some three weeks after the interview aired, the Queen wrote separately to Charles and to Diana asking them to arrange an early divorce 'in the best interests of the country'. And this from the woman who almost half a century before had told a Mother's Union rally: 'We can have no doubt that divorce and separation are responsible for some of the darkest evils in our society today.'

Towards Diana herself the Queen had never failed to demonstrate a degree of sympathy. In discussions over, among other things, the title of a divorced princess, Diana told Paul Burrell that the Queen continued to behave with 'sensitivity and kindness'. But she must have felt the deepest concern.

The divorce of the Waleses became final on 28 August 1996, just three months after the far more amicable divorce of the Yorks. But as an exercise in damage limitation it came too late.

Diana remained a thorn in the royal flesh, drawing headlines when she announced her retirement from public life. Charles was booed on public engagements; surveys indicated that only one person in three thought him fit to be king; and the Commonwealth countries also reacted to the decline in his credibility.

An academic had declared that 'something has died – the enchantment of the British people with the monarchy.' The events of the last years had seen the left-wing MP

Dennis Skinner declare that 'the Royal Family has just pressed the self-destruct button.' Another poll claimed that three out of four Britons believed the monarchy was crumbling.

On the positive side, the Queen's own approval rating in 1996 was still running at an enviable 73 per cent. Her Christmas message that year could reflect on a genuine new friendship with Nelson Mandela – 'the most gracious of men', as she described him (and one of the very few to call her Elizabeth).

All the same, bookies' odds on whether the Royal Family would survive into the twenty-first century were swinging between 100 to 1 and 5 to 1. The reputation of the British monarchy seemed to be enduring death by a thousand cuts – even headlines, in 1996, about the Queen Mother's embarrassingly large overdraft . . . But the real cataclysm had yet to strike.

South African President Nelson Mandela, making a state visit to London in 1996, after the ending of apartheid, was one world figure with whom the Queen struck up a particular rapport.

Fall and Rise

As 1997 dawned, it was clear that the problem of Diana would not simply fade away. During her eighteen months as a divorced woman she launched the anti-landmines campaign which stands as her lasting memorial. But she also conducted a largely private relationship with surgeon Hasnat Khan and a very public one with Dodi Fayed. And as she became ever more alienated from the Royal Family, Diana's increasingly eccentric behaviour (nuisance calls, rumoured affairs and New Age therapies) was discussed widely and crudely.

Sunday 31 August 1997 changed the royal world. If a divorced Princess of Wales had been a loose cannon, then her shocking death – in a Paris underpass, in a speeding car pursued by paparazzi – looked like being infinitely more damaging for the monarchy.

When the news came – first of Diana's accident, and then of her death from her injuries – the Royal Family were at Balmoral, on their annual holiday. It was the small hours of the morning, and the decision was taken not to wake Diana's sons to tell them of their terrible loss. From the start, William and Harry were the focus of the family's concern.

The decision to keep them at Balmoral – in comparative privacy, in the fresh air, away from the pressure of the media – is in itself hard to fault. And yet something went wrong. As national shock turned to anger it was as if Diana's death (so unexpected it seemed as though there must be some dark explanation behind it) provided a focus for all the mounting doubts about the Royal Family.

It was new Prime Minister Tony Blair who found the popular tribute. Diana had been, he said, 'the People's Princess'. The people's – not the monarchy's. The extraordinary outpouring of public grief was matched by an anger towards the only people who appeared not to care – the Royal Family.

The Queen and Prince Philip viewing the flowers left in tribute to Princess Diana outside the gates of Buckingham Palace. Their decision to leave Balmoral and return to London marked a turning point in the public mood.

The family's initial refusal to join in the public mourning was seen as evidence of hostility towards Diana. 'Speak to us, Ma'am,' demanded a *Mirror* newspaper headline. As the front page of the *Sun* put it: 'Every hour the palace remains empty adds to the public anger at what they perceive to be a snub to the People's Princess.' The *Daily Mail* published a front page asking whether it was 'time for the Queen to go'. Even *The Times* was dismayed that the church service at Balmoral immediately after Diana's death had special prayers for Charles and his sons, but no mention of their mother.

Some of the howls of complaint reflected a failure to understand royal protocol. It was taken as a sign of disrespect that there was no flag at half mast over Buckingham Palace – but in fact, traditionally the only flag ever flown there is the sovereign's own standard, and that only when the sovereign is in residence.

But the Royal Family, too, had failed in understanding. Even its own press office was dismayed by the family's apparent inability to appreciate the depth of public feeling. It was four days after Diana's death, Thursday 4 September, before wiser counsels prevailed. In the course of a forty-five-minute phone call with advisers, the Queen was persuaded to change her views. She has, as one of her private secretaries put it, 'ruthless common sense. She has the ability to move on.'

Once persuaded, she did the thing handsomely. The next day, after attending another church service at which prayers were asked for Diana, the Royal Family inspected the flowers which had been laid at Balmoral gates. Later that day the whole family would fly south to walk among the flowers left in London, talking to the crowds. And – from almost the moment of their return to London – royal popularity began once more to climb.

As the Union Jack – in defiance of all tradition – did fly at half mast over Buckingham Palace, the Queen prepared to broadcast live to the nation: 'What I say to you now as your Queen and as a grandmother, I say from my heart.' The words 'as a grandmother' may have been suggested by the Prime Minister's office, but when the Queen had been asked whether this speech was one she could deliver with conviction, she answered, yes, certainly – 'I believe every word.'

Diana 'was an exceptional and gifted human being', the Queen said in her speech. 'In good times and bad, she never lost her capacity to smile and laugh, nor to inspire others with her warmth and kindness. I admired and respected her . . . I for one believe there are lessons to be drawn from her life and from the extraordinary and moving reaction to her death. I share in your determination to cherish her memory.'

The next day, as Diana's cortège passed slowly through the streets on the way to her funeral at Westminster Abbey, to the heartbreaking tolling of a bell, the Queen spontaneously bowed her head as the coffin passed by.

The events of August and September might easily have set a tragic seal on 1997 (if not, indeed, on the monarchy). But in the longer run, Diana's death would prove to have lanced a boil, ending the divisive taking of sides and allowing the Royal Family to appear once more as a united entity. And the last few months of that very year would prove to have some surprises in store.

Less than three months after Diana's death the Queen and Prince Philip were due to celebrate their Golden Wedding anniversary. It was five years to the day since the fire that had ripped through Windsor Castle, and now the state rooms had been restored (the work, under Prince Philip's overall supervision, completed under budget and six months ahead of schedule) in time to be reopened for the occasion.

The day before the Golden Wedding, Prince Philip told guests at a Guildhall lunch hosted by the Lord Mayor that: 'tolerance is the one essential ingredient of any happy marriage . . . absolutely vital when the going gets difficult' – and that the wife seated beside him 'has the quality of tolerance in abundance'.

The next day the couple attended a service of thanksgiving at Westminster Abbey where they had married fifty years before. Elizabeth and Philip were surrounded not only by their children and grandchildren and a host of other foreign and homegrown royalty but, in a gesture of inclusiveness, by fifty other couples who had married in the same year as they.

In the ensuing 'people's banquet' organized by Tony Blair, the royal couple sat without distinction of rank among the 350 guests. When, in a speech afterwards, Blair hailed the Queen's timeless 'values of duty and service', it proved indeed to herald a new appreciation of those qualities. Blair praised her as 'a symbol of unity

The Golden Wedding anniversary of the Queen and Prince Philip, on 20 November 1997, found the Royal Family back on an upward path.

in a world of insecurity where nothing stays the same'. The Queen herself returned to the 'lessons to be drawn' theme on which she had touched three months before.

Both elected government and constitutional monarchy, she said, depended on the consent of the people. 'That consent, or lack of it, is expressed for you, Prime Minister, through the ballot box' – brutally, perhaps, but at least unmistakably. For the monarchy, by contrast 'the message is often harder to read, obscured as it can be by deference, rhetoric or the conflicting currents of public opinion. But read it we must.' (Prince Philip, presciently, many years before, had declared that the Royal Family was fighting an election every day.)

The Queen was alluding to Diana's death, but she also coupled herself with Philip, who had 'quite simply, been my strength and stay all these years'. 'I, and his whole family, and this and many other countries, owe him a debt greater than he would ever claim, or we shall ever know.' But, she added, 'It is you, if I may now speak to all of you directly, who have seen us through, and helped us to make our duty fun.'

When, some three weeks later, she and Philip stood on the quay of Portsmouth docks to say goodbye to *Britannia*, which had played such a huge part in the couple's 'fun', the Queen was seen to wipe away a tear. The yacht had been 'their floating home' as a lady-in-waiting said – their 'freedom', as a relative put it – and beyond that, it had meant a great deal to the Queen's father. In fact the decision to decommission and not replace the yacht which had served as something of a floating embassy, was already beginning to seem churlish.

Lessons were being learned on all sides. Within six months of Diana's death, the Palace had begun discreetly commissioning polls, the better to keep in tune with public opinion. Quietly, imperceptibly, they were taking on some of Diana's style – less formality, more visible inclusiveness. Tweaking engagements to allow the Queen to be more closely involved with those she met on visits, allowing her to appear as part of her people's lives, rather than simply as a spectacle or a spectator.

The polls now showed a mere 19 per cent of the population in favour of a republic, down from the higher figure reported in the days immediately after Diana's death. Life was back to normal. But everyone had seen how easily the tide could turn.

Saying goodbye to *Britannia*, as the royal yacht was decommissioned at
Portsmouth in December 1997, the Queen was seen to wipe away a tear.

A royal wedding always helps bring people together. In fact the wedding of Prince
Edward to Sophie Rhys-Jones on 19 June 1999 was a comparatively low-key affair,
held in St George's Chapel at Windsor, rather than in St Paul's like the Waleses, or
Westminster Abbey like the Yorks and the Phillips. But that, perhaps, was recognition
of the fact that no one wanted a huge fantasia just after seeing the sorry end of all
those apparent fairy stories. Indeed, this marriage would outlast those of Edward's
siblings, with the couple's children, Louise and James, born in 2003 and 2007.

The inner circle of the Royal Family had still to confront fresh difficulties. The Queen
Mother was now in her late nineties, though in remarkably good health for her years
and still even fulfilling a number of public engagements. Princess Margaret's health
was a matter of more acute concern. The sight of the former royal glamour girl
and partygoer in a wheelchair was a poignant reminder of just how many years
had passed.

The constraints of life as the Queen's sister had not made for happiness. Margaret had suffered a good deal of illness over the years, much of it inevitably connected with her smoking habit. In the early months of 1998 she suffered a mild stroke, though made a good recovery. Just a year later she scalded her feet, at her house in Mustique, badly enough to leave her with enduring difficulty in walking.

There was a loosening of political ties, too, within the nation's 'family', over which the Queen, whatever her thoughts, perforce presided. The Scottish Parliament was convened in 1998, the Welsh National Assembly established the same year. The reform of the House of Lords, which entailed the abolition of most hereditary peers, was a worrying precedent for a hereditary monarchy. But in November 1999, Australia – so often touted as by nature republican – voted by 55 per cent to 45 per cent to keep the Queen as its head of state.

True, as a new millennium dawned, at midnight on New Year's Eve 1999, the Queen looked glum as she clasped fingers with Prince Philip and Tony Blair for the singing of 'Auld Lang Syne'. Then again, the dissatisfaction with the Millennium Dome that her face seemed to display was shared by the rest of the country – a way in which she actually seemed more in touch than her government.

The monarchy was set on a determined path of reconciling past and present, and that was a theme the Queen herself readily understood. In her Christmas broadcast of 1999 she said: 'We can make sense of the future – if we understand the lessons of the past. Winston Churchill, my first Prime Minister, said that "the further backward you look, the further forward you can see."'

As we moved not only from one century, but from one millennium, to another, 'More than ever we are aware of being a tiny part of the infinite sweep of time.' And what better symbol of that sweep than an institution that had endured for centuries?

It seemed, as the veil of tears lifted, that Diana's legacy had been to jolt the royal establishment out of a decades-old complacency while giving its subjects a catharsis. The nation had vented its dissatisfaction and the Royal Family took it meekly. Promised to do better, effectively.

It helps that there have been (and the Palace, with its newly sharpened sensibilities, has taken full advantage) a huge number of events shared by the nation and their monarchy in the twenty years since Diana's death. The first year of the new millennium saw not only a milestone passed, and a visit to Australia after victory in the republican referendum, but the Queen Mother's one hundredth birthday.

A stream of celebrations ran through spring and summer, heading towards the great pageant in her honour on 19 July, on Horse Guards Parade in Whitehall. A march-past of the regiments with which she was particularly associated, the release of a hundred homing doves. A 'cavalcade of the century' – the Queen Mother's century – including everything from Pearly Kings and Queens to Enid Blyton's Noddy. Camels and racehorses, the Girls' Brigade and the Chelsea Pensioners, a page leading two of her own corgis while planes new and old flew overhead.

On the birthday itself, 4 August, after the royal postman had delivered the Queen's handwritten card to her mother (and its recipient, relishing the spectacle, had instructed her equerry to open it with his sword), the Queen Mother rode to Buckingham Palace through cheering crowds. It had been a great excuse for colourful ceremony. However, the next great royal events would be a trigger for a deeper emotion: sympathy.

Millennial Monarchy

The year 2002 – just a decade after the annus horribilis – was always going to be marked out as the fiftieth anniversary of the Queen's accession. In the event, it was also notable for two great losses in her life.

On 9 February, Princess Margaret died of cardiac problems following a stroke, her death by then a release from crippling ill health. It was obvious that the Queen Mother would not long survive her younger daughter. On 30 March she, too, died, with the Queen – summoned hastily from riding in Windsor Park – at her side.

Operation Tay Bridge (as the Queen Mother's funeral had been dubbed) had long been arranged, with her own active cooperation. Now the full state machinery swung into place.

Press opinion had held that there might be an embarrassing lack of public interest in the Queen Mother's obsequies – that this was the reason the period of official mourning was shorter than it would have been in earlier days. With hindsight it looks like an unnecessary pessimism, but the Palace must have been alarmed by the public apathy that had greeted Princess Margaret's death.

This time, however, opinion could not have been more wrong. The Queen Mother's coffin was driven from Windsor first to St James's Palace, for family and private visits, and then to Westminster Hall for a public lying in state. Beside her crown, with its legendary centrepiece of the Koh-i-Noor diamond, rested a single wreath of white roses and freesias that read 'In Loving Memory, Lilibet'.

More than a quarter of a million people lined the streets to see the coffin pass and waited to applaud the Queen herself as she drove back home after seeing her mother's catafalque put on public display. It was, the Queen said, one of the most moving things that had ever happened to her – and it was also a barometer that clearly showed better weather for the monarchy.

As the Queen Mother's body lay in state through a long weekend (she had died on Easter Saturday), people came in their hundreds of thousands, the queues stretching far down the other side of the Thames. The opening hours of Westminster Hall had to be extended to twenty-two hours a day. Perhaps the enthusiasm was as much about us, the people, and acknowledging our century, as it was about the woman who had come to represent it. To embody our hopes and fears, our triumphs and regrets, has always been the function of the monarchy.

The Queen is seen following her mother's coffin out of Westminster Abbey, after the funeral service of the Queen Mother on 9 April 2002. That spring had already seen the death of Princess Margaret.

As the Queen said in a speech the night before the funeral: 'Ever since my beloved mother died over a week ago, I have been deeply moved by the outpouring of affection which has accompanied her death . . . I thank you for the support you are giving me and my family as we come to terms with her death and the void she has left in our midst. I thank you also from my heart for the love you gave her during her life and the honour you now give her in death.'

On 9 April, after a service in Westminster Abbey, Queen Elizabeth the Queen Mother was buried at Windsor, beside her husband and with a casket containing the ashes of her younger daughter. It was the end of an era, but symptomatic, perhaps, of a new era for the Queen herself.

Both her mother and her sister, as she would say in her Christmas speech, had been 'very much part of my life and always gave me their support and encouragement'. But in some sense, nonetheless, this would prove to have been a moment of progression for the Queen – a moment when, as someone close to her put it, she 'stepped into the century'.

The Queen's Golden Jubilee in 2002 saw her in a more relaxed mood.

Her mother had always been a voice arguing against change, and one hard to resist. Now that voice was gone. Moreover it seemed as though she had herself taken on some of the characteristics of the relatives she had lost. The Queen Mother had been cast as the universally beloved one, Margaret as the glamorous one and Elizabeth as the steadfast one. Now she was all three.

The celebrations for Elizabeth II's Golden Jubilee went ahead as planned. On 4 June she travelled to St Paul's Cathedral in the Gold State Coach for a service of thanksgiving followed by lunch in the Guildhall. There she spoke of family continuity, 'taking this opportunity to mention the strength I draw from my own family. The Duke of Edinburgh has made an invaluable contribution to my life over these past fifty years.'

During the festivities the Queen, speaking at Westminster on 30 April, declared that if a Jubilee was a moment to define an age, then 'for me we must speak of change . . . Change has become a constant; managing it has become an expanding discipline. The way we embrace it defines our future.' As a sign of her determination to embrace change, the Queen invited Camilla Parker Bowles to the Golden Jubilee celebration.

In this warmer climate, it was once more possible to think about the future of the monarchy. As the Queen said when she opened the Hyde Park fountain in Diana's memory in July 2004: 'Of course there were difficult times, but memories mellow.' It was unthinkable that Charles, when the time came, should become king possessed

When the Queen visited Bushy Park for her Golden Jubilee, the welcome of the schoolchildren reflected a renewed public warmth towards the monarchy.

of a mistress rather than a wife. The Queen was wholly supportive when, on 9 April 2005, the Prince of Wales married his long-time love. There was again that willingness to change, to accept Charles's dictum that Camilla's presence in his life was 'non-negotiable'. And there was of course a concern for the happiness of a son who, as his mother must be aware, had often found his position difficult.

Sufficient time was felt to have passed since Diana's death for public hostility against Camilla Parker Bowles to have died down. The Queen had sounded out various Prime Ministers of the Commonwealth in the months before. Because Camilla had a first husband still living, the actual marriage had (since Prince Charles wished to marry at Windsor, rather than taking Princess Anne's Scottish way out of the difficulty) to be a civil ceremony in Windsor registry office, which the Queen as Supreme Governor of the Church of England felt it was inappropriate to attend. But she was there at the service of dedication in St George's Chapel which followed.

At the wedding reception the Queen first announced that Hedgehunter had won that day's Grand National and then, linking the couple with the fences of that famous race: 'They have overcome Becher's Brook and the Chair and all kinds of obstacles.

When Prince Charles married Camilla Parker Bowles in April 2005 the Queen's expression showed her pleasure. 'Welcome to the winner's enclosure', she told the couple.

The Queen smiling at the crowds out in Windsor to celebrate her 80th birthday.

They have come through and I'm very proud and wish them well. My son is home and dry with the woman he loves. Welcome to the winner's enclosure.' A racing woman could go no further.

When Prince Charles organized a family dinner for the Queen's eightieth birthday the next year he spoke of his 'darling Mama' – through all the years 'a figure of reassuring calm and dependability'. At an official lunch at the Mansion House she herself noted that: 'As one gets older, birthdays seem to come round quicker; they are therefore less obvious excuses for wider celebration than personal moments to

The Queen's 80th birthday was greeted as a cause for national, as well as family, rejoicing.

count one's blessings. As Groucho Marx once said: "Anyone can get old – all you have to do is live long enough."'

In 2006 the Queen was presented in a new light – as played by Helen Mirren in the eponymous movie. Though the portrayal of other family members of the Royal Family was unflattering – and insiders say it shows only the suppressed public Queen rather than the sparky private one – those who know her say that essentially the picture rings true.

Certainly in the end *The Queen* must be counted as more blessing than curse. It showed an Elizabeth whose natural compassion was at war with her rigid sense of duty, who had early been forced, by her father's untimely death, into a lifetime of rigid formality.

At the Academy Awards ceremony in February 2007, Helen Mirren, accepting the Best Actress Oscar, said that: 'For fifty years, and more, Elizabeth Windsor has maintained her dignity, her sense of duty – and her hairstyle. She's had her feet planted firmly on the ground, her hat on her head, her handbag on her arm, and she's weathered many, many storms. I salute her courage and her consistency . . . Ladies and gentlemen, I give you – the Queen!'

New Generations

In the second decade of the twenty-first century the Royal Family has seemed firmly set on an upward path. The Queen's sheer longevity – once seen as a problem – has proved to be a strength. She is firmly established as National Treasure Number One, while Diana's sons are seen at once as flying the flag of royal tradition, and carrying on their mother's legacy.

When the engagement of His Royal Highness Prince William of Wales to Miss Catherine Middleton was announced in November 2010, it looked as though the modern age had finally hit the monarchy. So it had, in a way, with a future heir to the throne marrying a woman rooted firmly in the British middle classes.

But in another way – as the Queen is perhaps realistic enough to have known – the match follows the tradition of centuries. Royal marriages always used to be about cementing an alliance – with some foreign power, historically. The difference is that in the twenty-first century, it is an alliance with the British people that the Royal Family needs most urgently.

When William and Kate married on 29 April the following year, and assumed the titles of Duke and Duchess of Cambridge, more than two billion people worldwide – almost a third of the world's population – are estimated to have watched the wedding (far outstripping the 750 million who watched the wedding of William's parents). The atmosphere was overwhelmingly inclusive. The guest list cut down on foreign dignitaries to make way for such old friends as the landlord of the Old Boot Inn near the Middletons' home village of Bucklebury in Berkshire.

That was definitely an innovation – a change from Charles and Diana's wedding – which had the Queen's express approval. Prince William has described how Palace officials at first handed him a proposed guest list with almost 777 names on it, all of people he didn't know. It was the Queen herself who told them that was 'ridiculous', they should start with their own friends – that it was their day. There is a strong sense that she approves of Kate Middleton – interested less in her comparatively humble origins than in the fact that she comes from a stable and loving family.

As the Bishop of London declared, 'In a sense every wedding is a royal wedding with the bride and groom as king and queen of creation.' But this day was especially enchanting, with a Westminster Abbey full of trees, a verger caught on camera cartwheeling down the aisle, and the young couple taking an evening drive past the last of the camping crowds in a vintage car with an L-plate tacked on to it by William's best man, Prince Harry.

The popularity of his parents and children might easily have left Prince Charles out in the cold. But he, too, is a more popular figure than he used to be. His visit of reconciliation to Northern Ireland is a case in point. That he should, after the distress he suffered over Lord Mountbatten's death, engage with the peace process to end the Troubles did much to reclaim for him that moral high ground which has long been presented as the justification for the Royal Family and which, back in the 1990s, they seemed to have lost so completely. The Queen herself made a historic visit to Dublin in 2011 – the first by a British monarch for one hundred years – delighting her audience with a few words of Gaelic.

In a happier second marriage, Prince Charles's relations with his family, too, seem easier. In her 2008 Christmas broadcast the Queen spoke of the 'blessing, comfort and support' she and her husband gained from Charles, just turned sixty. In a speech a few weeks earlier she had described their comfort in knowing 'that into his care are safely entrusted the guiding principles of public service and duty'.

The Diamond Jubilee of 2012 saw the Prince's praise for 'Mummy'. It was a very different tone from the speeches of earlier years, and the Royal Family had come a long way. How to mark the Diamond Jubilee had been discussed long in advance, and far around the world. This was, after all, a historic event, with Queen Victoria the only previous British monarch to have remained so long on the throne. (And with future sovereigns likely to come to the throne at a much greater age, we will not readily see these jubilees again.) It soon became apparent that the 2,012 beacons originally planned to be lit across the Commonwealth in no way matched up to the real appetite for celebration. In the end (after the first beacon was lit in Tonga with a coconut sheath torch) there would prove to be more than four thousand in the UK alone.

The Queen's own contribution to the debate comprised two firm opinions: that the use of public funds should be minimized, and that the public should not be 'forced to celebrate'. The first was resolved by the large number of projects funded by private sponsorship; and about the second she need not have worried.

Events extended through the spring and summer. (Understandably, the Queen has always preferred to limit celebration of the February day on which she actually acceded to the throne. To her, after all, it was the day on which her father died.) Her children and grandchildren embarked on a series of visits on her behalf to the Commonwealth countries – visits she would, at a younger age, have undertaken in person. The occasion was also marked with commemorative coins and stamps, a special lottery grant, a time capsule and the renaming of a stretch of Antarctica.

Perhaps the most 'English' celebration was the tea party held by a group of climbers atop a Canadian Arctic mountain; the most international, a special Google Doodle. The most traditionally monarchical was the lunch the Queen hosted at Windsor for more than twenty current or former monarchs.

Especially interesting was the Jubilee Hour initiative by which, in recognition of the Queen's sixty years on the throne, organizations or individuals could pledge sixty minutes of their time to help their local community. Some 2.75 million hours were pledged. As the Buckingham Palace statement put it: 'It was the Queen's hope that her Diamond Jubilee would provide an opportunity for communities, groups and individuals to come together in a way that they would not otherwise be able to do.'

The bulk of the Jubilee events – formal celebrations in London, and street parties around the country – were concentrated over one four-day-long bank holiday weekend in June. On Sunday 3 June, the River Thames Diamond Jubilee Pageant was held, the largest flotilla of boats the river had seen in 350 years – barges, cruisers, skiffs, Dunkirk 'little boats' – marred only by terrible weather. The next day brought a picnic for ten thousand before the Diamond Jubilee Concert, which featured

The Queen's Diamond Jubilee was marked by a service of thanksgiving in St Paul's Cathedral on 5 June 2015. Elizabeth II is only the second British monarch to reach this anniversary, the first being Queen Victoria.

performers representing musical styles from throughout the Queen's reign, including Shirley Bassey, Grace Jones and Kylie Minogue.

On 5 June, there was a national service of thanksgiving at St Paul's, to which the Queen was accompanied by Charles and Camilla, the Duke and Duchess of Cornwall. They were joined by a host of younger royals. But it seemed particularly poignant that she had to attend this ceremony without her husband by her side.

After the river pageant Prince Philip gallantly stood in the open air by his wife, tapping his foot to music as the royal barge steered up the Thames through drenching rain. The year before, the Queen had made him the nation's Lord High Admiral, a title she herself had borne until then. However, the next day Philip was suddenly admitted to hospital. The Queen had to go through the rest of the celebrations without him, and it seemed all too clear a symbol of what may be ahead. The Duke of Edinburgh, almost five years older than his wife, was seemingly in less robust health than she.

Prince Philip, on the death of her mother and sister, had become the only person who could speak to the Queen on terms of equality, who could give her the affectionate nickname of 'Bet', for 'Lilibet'. In the spring of 2017, news that he would be retiring from public life sparked a wave of concern, and of interest in what had become the longest royal marriage in British history.

The Duchess of Cambridge has spoken of the importance for the Queen of having the support of a husband not only on public occasions, but 'behind closed doors', saying truly that having to fulfill her role alone would be 'a very, very lonely place to be'. The world knows Elizabeth II is a woman who meets with stoicism whatever comes. But the loss of her husband at her side could only be immense (the more so since many of the network of cousins and long-serving courtiers on whom she long-relied upon have already predeceased her).

The Queen has, however, always been temperamentally attuned to looking at the future in a positive way. Recent years have seen her engage – at least nominally – with the new media generation, sending a token tweet and observing the activities of her grandchildren on Facebook. The opening ceremony of the 2012 London Olympic Games saw her almost making showbusiness history as the first monarch to appear in a James Bond movie sketch. The Queen herself was seen being escorted out of the Palace by Daniel Craig, in his character of 007 – and then, for one delirious second, we seemed to see the 86-year-old monarch parachuting down from the stadium roof. Sportingly, the real Queen made no difficulty at all about agreeing to wear the same outfit as the stunt double who actually leapt from the helicopter.

But there is, of course, a new generation coming into the Royal Family. The Queen's first great-grandchild, Savannah Phillips, had been born in 2010, to Princess Anne's son Peter. In December 2012, news that the Duchess of Cambridge was pregnant triggered a rush to change the rules of succession laid down more than three hundred years before – notably, the rule that a male heir would always be given precedence over a female.

The Queen was by no means averse to this change. In March and October the preceding year, her speeches had twice referred to the fact that the Commonwealth was that year celebrating women as 'agents of change', which 'reminds us of the potential in our societies that is yet to be fully unlocked, and it encourages us to find ways to allow girls and women to play their full part.' It was a theme to which she would return.

In the event, the birth of Prince George on 22 July 2013 made the succession changes irrelevant in the immediate future. But Princess Charlotte, born on 2 May 2015, will continue to follow her elder brother George in the succession rather than being displaced by any future boy. And the new legislation will endure – for as long as the (now modernized) monarchy does.

The formal announcement of Prince George's birth was placed, by custom, on an easel outside Buckingham Palace. But the next day Prince William, having taken paternity leave from his job as an RAF search and rescue pilot, was seen strapping his son into a baby seat – just like any other father – before driving his new family down to Kate's parents in Bucklebury and privacy.

When, on 9 September 2015, Elizabeth II became the longest-reigning monarch in British history, it seemed a kind of national victory. Her reign had been, Prime Minister David Cameron told the House of Commons, a 'golden thread running through three post-war generations'.

On 23 September 1896, Queen Victoria had been able to note in her diary that 'This is the day on which I have reigned longer, by a day, than any English sovereign.' It will

By the time the Queen celebrated her 90th birthday in 2016, the family party on the balcony of Buckingham Palace included Prince George, now third in line to the throne, and baby Princess Charlotte.

be many years before we see the diaries this Queen has kept religiously at the end of each day. But her tone will probably be more pragmatic than that of her predecessor.

On 9 September she – with her husband and Scotland's First Minister Nicola Sturgeon – were in the Scottish Borders to open a new railway. Her speech was a blend of grace and bluntness as she acknowledged the many messages she had received. 'Inevitably, a long life can pass by many milestones. My own is no exception. But I thank you all . . . So now to the business in hand.'

A little more than six months later came the Queen's ninetieth birthday (to be followed, in February 2017, by another milestone: her Sapphire Jubilee). It was, again, a time of huge public celebration. But 2016 ended with widespread concern at the Queen's non-appearance at Christmas festivities – though she eventually recovered from her cold – and with the announcement that the younger members of the family would be taking on more of her responsibilities.

Discreetly, the Palace let it be known that the Queen might be spending less time in

At 90, Elizabeth II is not only the oldest, but the longest-reigning monarch in British history. Time and again, her nation has cause to celebrate another milestone passed, be it jubilee, birthday or anniversary . . .

Buckingham Palace and more at her other residences, where the quieter pace of life is more suitable for a nonagenarian. There was a sense that this marked some kind of a punctuation mark in the long history of the Queen's reign.

For many years, the question has been asked of whether she would ever consider an abdication. After all, 'Never Say Never' might be the motto of the monarchy throughout Elizabeth II's reign. But courtiers have always insisted 'the A-word' cannot even be mentioned in the Queen's presence – that it is something the Queen would consider a dereliction of duty.

When an Archbishop of Canterbury informed her of his retirement, she remarked that, of course, retirement from her job was not an option. She would never break that vow she made for her twenty-first birthday. And she has always been deeply aware of the monarchical role as a sacred, almost a priestly, duty.

The Queen on Stage and Screen

There have been dozens of fictional glimpses of the Queen, from the ridiculous to the sublime. Countless biopics about the Royal Family's story, impressions and comedy shows.

One actress quite literally made a career out of impersonating the Queen. Lookalike Jeannette Charles lent a touch of royal ridicule to everything from a National Lampoon movie to a Naked Gun and an Austin Powers. When she appeared as the Queen in an episode of *Big Brother*, at least one contestant thought it was for real. Jennifer Saunders, Eddie Izzard and Vanessa Redgrave have all voiced animated versions of her and *Saturday Night Live* has seen several incarnations of the Queen over the years, created by performers including Joan Cusack and Fred Armisen. Almost a quarter of a century after the BBC's satirical show of the early 1960s *That Was the Week that Was*, *Spitting Image* took up the mocking theme with even less deference. But other dramas have attempted to portray the Queen more seriously, at various stages of her life.

In *The King's Speech* she was seen as a child just old enough to be aware of the consequences of her uncle's abdication. In *A Royal Night Out*, Sarah Gadon played the young Princess escaping the Palace to join the crowds to celebrate VE Day. In Channel 4's 2009 mini series *The Queen* five different actresses – Emilia Fox, Samantha Bond, Susan Jameson, Barbara Flynn and Diana Quick – were seen on five consecutive nights, catching her at five different moments of her reign.

Rosemary Leach has played the Queen three times over the years in different TV plays, notably in *Tea with Betty*, which imagines her visiting a single mum on a council estate. Penelope Wilton played her in the children's film *The BFG* in 2016. Even Emma Thompson has played her, in *Walking the Dogs*, a 2012 TV film dramatizing the episode when, in 1982, Michael Fagan broke into her bedroom at Buckingham Palace. On stage, in 1988, Prunella Scales portrayed the Queen in Alan Bennett's one-act play

A Question of Attribution, about the exposure of her art expert Anthony Blunt as a Communist spy. Scales reprised the role for the 1991 TV adaptation of the play (and she would also make an uncredited screen appearance as the Queen in the 2003 spy spoof *Johnny English*, besides voicing an animated version in *Freddie* as F.R.O.7.)

More recently, Kristin Scott Thomas appeared on stage as the Queen in a 2015 revival of *The Audience*, Peter Morgan's imagining of the Queen's audiences with her various Prime Ministers. Scott Thomas succeeded Helen Mirren who – seven years after she first walked in Queen Elizabeth II's shoes – took the role in the West End and on Broadway, and added a Tony to the Oscar she had already won for her portrayal.

For Helen Mirren is of course familiar to most of us from the 2006 film *The Queen*, directed by Stephen Frears from Peter Morgan's screenplay.

Helen Mirren's would, until just recently, have had to be called the single most important portrayal of the Queen. Mirren studied photos and videos, the Queen's patterns of speech and the way she holds her head. Peter Morgan reported that as the shoot went on, crew members began to behave around the actress almost as though she were the real monarch. The half-Russian Mirren herself was brought up an anti-monarchist, but says her parents might have taken a more benign view today – as does she.

'People have woken up to the truth that was always there,' Mirren said when *The Queen* came out. 'I think the Windsors

Helen Mirren's sympathetic portrayal of Elizabeth II in Stephen Frears' film *The Queen* won her an Academy Award.

Claire Foy, in the first two seasons of *The Crown*, is the latest in a very long line of actresses to take on the sovereign's role.

have served us, if that's what you want, fantastically – she particularly. I think the Queen has served us incredibly well.' Mirren may not consider herself to be a monarchist, but she is a 'queenist' – and it sounds as if the other actress to inhabit the role as thoroughly as Dame Helen may feel much the same way.

Claire Foy, who plays the Queen at the start of her reign in the first, ten-episode, series of Netflix's *The Crown*, says that she had always taken the Royal Family for granted – but no longer. 'They work their socks off, and Elizabeth's been working since she was twenty-five every single day of her life. It's a never-ending job, and I think she's done it really well . . . She's a check and a balance on the government. [The Royal Family has] done an extraordinary job.'

The Crown – the third royal outing for Peter Morgan, the man who wrote *The Queen* and *The Audience* – was touted as the most expensive TV drama ever, costing a rumoured £100 million, and has been hailed not only for its lavish production values but for historical accuracy. It won Golden Globes not only for Best Television Series but for Claire Foy in the leading role. Another five series are now planned, taking the story up towards the present day, with two other actresses expected to play the Queen at later stages of her life.

Throughout his two-and-a-half years of research, Morgan avoided any contact with a Palace keen always to ensure that the monarchy is shown in a flattering light. But they need not have worried. Morgan sees his Queen as a good, a very good, person 'who has given her life for her country'.

'She's good at the job because she takes it seriously and in doing so gives it meaning,' Morgan says. 'If you got a team of scientists together, you couldn't create a better queen.' Winston Churchill said very much the same, in the year she acceded to the throne: 'All the film people in the world, if they had scoured the globe, could not have found anyone so suited to the part.'

Claire Foy and Matt Smith portray the Queen and Prince Philip in the Netflix series, *The Crown*.

Epilogue: Legacy

The last third of the Queen's long life has seen dramatic changes for the House of Windsor. The monarchy's spectacular fall in popularity and prestige has been followed by a phoenix-like resurgence. As Elizabeth II moved into her tenth decade, she could rest assured that she would leave behind a formidable legacy.

The Queen's ninetieth birthday came at a strange and significant time in her country's history. A moment when Britain's proposed exit from the European Union could arguably restore to the monarch a greater sovereignty. But a moment, too, when dissatisfaction over the decision to leave could threaten the union of the kingdoms.

There are questions as to what might happen in the years ahead – not least to the Commonwealth, of which Prince Charles will not automatically become head. Membership of the Commonwealth has grown from eight member states when Elizabeth came to the throne, to a present tally of fifty-two.

The Queen herself always has shown a steely determination to preserve the integrity of her Commonwealth 'family', even when to do so set her at odds with her ministers, or when it meant her acknowledging some otherwise unacceptable regimes. But when her talismanic figure, living reminder of a shared past, is gone the future may be less certain – just as some of the dozen or more territories happy to recognize her as head of state may then decide to choose a head of their own nationality.

Elizabeth and her fellow 'Diamond Queen', Victoria, faced the same challenges – as woman, wife, mother and monarch – and there can be no doubt that the modern monarch has faced them with far greater constancy. Much credit for the recent rebirth of the House of Windsor has surely to be given to the Queen herself. Whatever mistakes may have been made in the past, Elizabeth II has emerged as a figure distinct from them, powerful in her very immutability.

Her act will be a hard one to follow – hard for a series of male heirs, particularly.

The English, it is said, like queens – Elizabeth I, Victoria, Elizabeth II – and it may be truer than ever today. The role of the modern constitutional monarch may even be one a woman can occupy more easily. Mother of the nation, effectively . . . The authoritarian image of a king as father figure may not play as readily. Yet Elizabeth II may well reflect that the great achievement of her last years has been to leave the throne secure to the heirs of her body.

Prince William spoke recently and warmly of his grandmother's personality. He mentioned the Queen's 'kindness and sense of humour, her innate sense of calm and perspective and her love of family and home'. He hinted, too, at the hope that she held out for the future of the monarchy. In regular meetings, while he was still at school, she trained and encouraged him as George V and Queen Mary did her.

Flanked by her eldest son and heir Prince Charles, her eldest grandson Prince William and his son, George, the Queen can reflect with pride that between them they have steered the monarchy back into safe waters and have a long line of successors to come.

The Prince's theme was one of change tempered by continuity – both for the Crown and for the country. 'All of us who will inherit the legacy of my grandmother's reign and generation need to do all we can to celebrate and learn from her story.'

Bibliography

Bates, Stephen, *Royalty Inc.: Britain's Best-Known Brand* (Aurum Press, 2015)

Bedell Smith, Sally, *Elizabeth the Queen: The Woman Behind the Throne* (Penguin, 2012

Bradford, Sarah, *Queen Elizabeth II: Her Life in Our Times* (Viking, 2011)

Brandreth, Gyles, *Philip and Elizabeth: Portrait of a Marriage* (Century, 2004)

Debrett's *The Queen: The Diamond Jubilee* (Simon & Schuster, 2012)

Eastoe, Jane, *Elizabeth: Reigning in Style* (Pavilion Books, 2012)

Guitaut, Caroline de, *The Queen's Coronation 1953: The Official Souvenir Album* (Royal Collection Trust, 2013)

Lacey, Robert, *Majesty: Elizabeth II and the House of Windsor* (Sphere, 1979) and *A Brief Life of the Queen* (Gerald Duckworth & Co Ltd, 2012)

Longford, Elizabeth, *Elizabeth R: A Biography* (Weidenfeld & Nicolson, 1983)

Marr, Andrew, *The Diamond Queen: Elizabeth II and Her People* (Macmillan, 2012)

Pimlott, Ben, *The Queen: Elizabeth II and the Monarchy* (HarperCollins, 2002)

Seward, Ingrid, *The Queen's Speech: An Intimate Portrait of the Queen in Her Own Words* (Simon & Schuster, 2015)

Shawcross, William, *Queen Elizabeth the Queen Mother: The Official Biography* (Macmillan, 2009)

Weir, Alison; Kate Williams; Sarah Gristwood; Tracy Borman, *The Ring and the Crown: A History of Royal Weddings 1066–2011* (Hutchinson, 2011)

Williams, Kate, *Young Elizabeth: The Making of Our Queen* (Weidenfeld & Nicolson, 2012)

Picture Credits

Alamy Stock Photo/Keystone Pictures USA 6a; Classic Image 21, 24; SWNS 38; Everett Collection Inc. 55; Trinity Mirror/Mirrorpix 91; Keystone Pictures USA 95; Rebecca Naden/Reuters 96; Toby Melville/Reuters 140a; AF Archive 151. **Camera Press**/Baron 4; Jason Bell 155. **Getty Images**/Bettmann front cover above; Printer Collector front cover below left; Bentley Archive/Popperfoto front cover below right; Paul Popper/Popperfoto back cover above; Hulton Archive/Stringer back cover below; © Hulton-Deutsch Collection/CORBIS/Corbis via Getty Images 6bl; Stringer/AFP 6br; Popperfoto 8; Oli Scarff 12; Central Press 13; Fox Photos 15; Popperfoto 16, 18al; Paul Popper/Popperfoto 18ar; Keystone-France/Gamma-Keystone via Getty Images 18b; Lisa Sheridan/Studio Lisa 20; George Rinhart/Corbis via Getty Images 23; Paul Popper/Popperfoto 25; Marcus Adams/Paul Popper/Popperfoto 26; The Print Collector/Print Collector 27; Popperfoto 29; © Hulton-Deutsch Collection/CORBIS/Corbis via Getty Images 31; Lisa Sheridan/Studio Lisa 33; Popperfoto 35; Keystone/Hulton Archive 36; © Hulton-Deutsch Collection/CORBIS/Corbis via Getty Images 37; © CORBIS/Corbis via Getty Images 40-41; Popperfoto 40b; Paul Popper/Popperfoto 47; Popperfoto 48; Hulton Archive 56; Popperfoto 59; Paul Popper/Popperfoto 60; Dmitri Kessel/The LIFE Picture Collection 61l; Fox Photos 61r; Picture Post/IPC Magazines/Hulton Archive 65; Keystone-France/Gamma-Keystone via Getty Images 67; Keystone 72a; Tim Graham 72bl, 72br; ullstein bild via Getty Images 75; Keystone-France/Gamma-Rapho via Getty Images 76; Quadrillion/CORBIS/Corbis via Getty Images 77; Tim Graham 78; George Freston/Fox Photos 80; Keystone 81; Hulton Archive 82a; Tim Graham 82b; Keystone 83; Paul Popper/Popperfoto 84; Hulton Archive/Keystone 85; Rolls Press/Popperfoto 87; Bettmann 88; Rolls Press/Popperfoto 89; Hulton Archive/Central Press 90; Hulton Archive 93; Bentley Archive/Popperfoto 94; Anwar Hussein 97, 98, 99, 100; Popperfoto 101a, 101b, 102; Fox Photos/Hulton Archive 103; Lichfield 106; Tim Graham 107; Lichfield 109; Central Press 110; Serge Lemoine 111; Lefteris Pitarakis/AFP 112; Popperfoto 113; Tim Graham 114; Adrian Dennis/AFP 116ar; Max Mumby/Indigo 116b; © Pool Photograph/Corbis/Corbis via Getty Images 121; Tim Graham 122, 124; Julian Parker/UK Press via Getty Images 127; © Pool Photograph/Corbis/Corbis via Getty Images 131; Tim Graham 133; Adrian Dennis/AFP 137; Jeff Overs/BBC News & Current Affairs via Getty Images 138; Anwar Hussein 139; MJ Kim 140b; Pool/Anwar Hussein Collection 141; Murray Sanders - WPA Pool 145; Max Mumby/Indigo 147; Chris Jackson 148; Arthur Edwards - WPA Pool 149; © Pool Photograph/Corbis/Corbis via Getty Images 151. **Mary Evans**/Hardy Amies London 11; © Illustrated London News Ltd. 39, 71. **REX/Shutterstock**/Tim Rooke 116al; David Hartley 120; 129; Netflix 152. **Shutterstock**/Kilroy79 1. **Victoria and Albert Museum, London**/© Cecil Beaton 17, 54.

Index

Page numbers in *italics* refer to illustrations

Author's Note

'The English' – said one of Elizabeth II's female ancestors – 'like queens.' She might have added that the Scots, the Welsh and a good many others do, too. This queen, Elizabeth II, has been an important part of the backdrop to so many lives across the British Isles and beyond. As a child, I was taken to watch the Silver Jubilee procession from a balcony above the Mall. As a young woman, I went to a Buckingham Palace garden party. As an adult, I've toured Windsor, Sandringham, Holyroodhouse, and dined aboard Britannia, I've commented on royal affairs for numerous TV news programmes and documentary series, and perched high in Broadcasting House while the 2011 royal wedding unfolded, as one of the team providing live coverage for BBC Radio 4.

I have also written books about Elizabeth II's famous predecessor Elizabeth I, and newspaper articles comparing her to her fellow Diamond Queen Victoria. (A comparison, I may say, out of which our present queen emerges very favourably!) Of course, a queen regnant in the sixteenth or even the nineteenth century occupied a very different position to her twenty-first-century successor. But all the same, what strikes me is how many of the problems – and the patterns – continue down to the present day.

When Elizabeth I died in 1603, after what was then a notably long reign, a contemporary wrote that the shock of the news 'took away hearts from millions.' A whole nation had been 'brought up under her wing' – had 'never shouted any ave but for her name.' You don't need to be an ardent monarchist to derive the same sense of continuity from Elizabeth II. When she acceded to the throne in the spring of 1952, Winston Churchill declared that 'Famous have been the reigns of our queens.' The reign of Queen Elizabeth II will be famous above all for the changes it has seen. But as in the spring of 2017 it reached an extraordinary tally of sixty-five years, she herself remains an iconic figure of reassuring stability.